COOKBC

MW01674761

SNACKS AND SQUARE 2022

100 RECIPES DIPPED IN CHOCOLATE, FROSTING, MARSHMALLOWS, CANDY AND FRUIT FOR YOUR PARTIES

SUSAN MASON

© Copyright 2022

- All rights reserved.

The following Book is reproduced below with the goal of providing information that is as accurate and reliable as possible. Regardless, purchasing this Book can be seen as consent to the fact that both the publisher and the author of this book are in no way experts on the topics discussed within and that any recommendations or suggestions that are made herein are for entertainment purposes only. Professionals should be consulted as needed prior to undertaking any of the action endorsed herein.

This declaration is deemed fair and valid by both the American Bar Association and the Committee of Publishers Association and is legally binding throughout the United States.

Furthermore, the transmission, duplication, or reproduction of any of the following work including specific information will be considered an illegal act irrespective of if it is done electronically or in print. This extends to creating a secondary or tertiary copy of the work or a recorded copy and is only allowed with the express written consent from the Publisher. All additional right reserved.

The information in the following pages is broadly considered a truthful and accurate account of facts and as such, any inattention, use, or misuse of the information in question by the reader will render any resulting actions solely under their purview. There are no scenarios in which the publisher or the original author of this work can be in any fashion deemed liable for any hardship or damages that may befall them after undertaking information described herein.

Additionally, the information in the following pages is intended only for informational purposes and should thus be thought of as universal. As befitting its nature, it is presented without assurance regarding its prolonged validity or interim quality. Trademarks that are mentioned are done without written consent and can in no way be considered an endorsement from the trademark holder.

Sommario

INTRODUCTION

What is a brownie? Brownie is a square or rectangular chocolate baked dessert. Brownies come in a variety of forms and may be either fudgy or cakey, depending on their density. They may include nuts, frosting, cream cheese, chocolate chips, or other ingredients.

What are fat bombs? Fat bombs are low carb and sugar-free sweet treats, usually made with coconut oil, coconut butter, cream cheese, avocado, and/or nut butter. Pretty much, anything high fat, sugar-free and low carb can be made to become a fat bomb.

What are dessert balls?Basically, it is a rich sweet confection made with sugar and often flavored or combined with fruits or nuts.What could possibly be better than a decadent dessert? One that comes in the shape of a ball!

From here on, baking up from scratch, a batch of brownies or fat bomb or a dessert ball will be as easy as reaching for the boxed stuff, thanks to these recipes.

Let's dive in!

BROWNIES & FUDGE

a) Chocolate hazelnut brownies

Ingredients:

- 1 cup unsweetened cocoa powder
- 1 cup all-purpose flour
- 1 tsp. baking soda
- ¼ tsp. salt
- 2 TBSP. unsalted butter
- 8 TBSP. butter
- 1½ cups dark brown sugar, firmly packed
- 4 large eggs
- 2 tsp. vanilla extract
- ½ cup milk chocolate chips
- ½ cup semisweet chocolate chips
- ½ cup toasted hazelnuts, chopped

a) Heat the oven to 340°F (171°C). Lightly coat a 9×13-inch (23×33cm) baking pan with nonstick cooking spray and set aside. In a medium bowl, combine unsweetened cocoa powder, all-purpose flour, baking soda, and salt. Set aside.

b) In a double boiler over low heat, melt together unsalted butter and butter. Once melted, remove from heat and stir in dark brown sugar. Pour butter-sugar mixture into flour mixture and stir to combine.

c) In a large bowl, beat eggs and vanilla extract with an electric mixer at medium speed for 1 minute. Slowly add in butter-flour mixture and mix for 1 more minute until just combined. Add milk chocolate chips, semisweet chocolate chips, and hazelnuts, and beat for a few seconds to quickly distribute.

d) Transfer mixture to the prepared pan and bake for 23 to 25 minutes or until top looks dark and dry. Cool completely in the pan before cutting into 24 pieces and moving to a plate.

e) Storage: Keep tightly wrapped in plastic wrap in the refrigerator for 4 to 5 days or in the freezer for 4 to 5 months.

b) Chocolate Brownies

Ingredients:

10. 1/4 cup butter
11. 1/4 cup normal butter
12. 2 eggs
13. 1 teaspoon vanilla extract
14. 1/3 cup unsweetened cocoa powder
15. 1/2 cup all-purpose flour
16. 1/4 teaspoon salt
17. 1/4 teaspoon baking powder

For the Frosting:

- 3 tablespoons butter, softened
- 1 teaspoon butter, softened
- 1 tablespoon honey
- 1 teaspoon vanilla extrac t
- 1 cup confectioners‘ sugar

Directions:

- Preheat oven to 330 degrees F.
- Grease and flour an 8-inch square pan.
- In a large saucepan, on very low heat, melt 1/4 cup butter and 1/4 cup butter.
- Remove from heat, and stir in sugar, eggs and 1 teaspoon vanilla. Beat in 1/3 cup cocoa, 1/2 cup flour, salt and baking powder. Spread batter into prepared pan.
- Bake in preheated oven for 25 to 30 minutes. Do not overcook.

For Frosting:

Combine 3 tablespoons softened butter and 1 teaspoon butter; add tablespoons cocoa, honey, 1 teaspoon vanilla extract, and 1 cup confectioners‘ sugar. Stir until smooth

c) Rocky Road Brownies

Yield: 12 brownies

Ingredients:

- 1/2 cup cannabis-infused butter
- 1/8 cup butter
- 2 ounces unsweetened chocolate
- 4 ounces bittersweet or semisweet chocolate
- 3/4 cup all-purpose flou r
- 1/2 teaspoon salt
- 1 cup granulated sugar
- 2 large eggs
- 1 teaspoon vanilla extract
- 3/4 cup toasted almond slices
- 1 cup miniature marshmallows

Directions:

1. Preheat the oven to 350 degrees F. Line an 8-inch square baking pan with aluminum foil, and grease foil with either butter or vegetable shortening.
2. Melt the cannabutter, butter and chocolates over low heat in a medium saucepan stirring frequently. Set aside to cool for 5 minutes.
3. Stir together the flour and salt; set aside.
4. Stir the sugar into the melted cannabutter until well combined.
5. Beat in the eggs and vanilla and continue mixing until well incorporated.
6. Mix in the flour and salt until just incorporated.
7. Reserve 1/2 cup of the brownie batter, and spread the remainder into the prepared pan.
8. Bake batter in the pan for about 20 minutes. While it is baking, prepare the topping by stirring together the reserved batter with the toasted almonds and marshmallows
9. After batter in pan has baked for 20 minute, remove from oven.
10. Spread topping over par-baked brownies and return to oven. Bake for about 10 more minutes or until marshmallows are browned and a toothpick inserted in the center comes out with just a few moist crumbs clinging to it

11. Let cool in pan before using the foil to lift out the brownies and slice.

d) Peanut and Jelly Fudge

Ingredients:

- Maple syrup, ¾ cup
- Vanilla extract, 1 teaspoon
- Peanuts, 1/3 cup, chopped
- Peanut butter, ¾ cup
- Dried cherries, 1/3 cup, diced
- Chocolate protein powder, ½ cup

Method:

- Chop peanuts and cherries and keep aside.
- Heat maple syrup on low then pour over peanut butter in a bowl. Mix until smooth.
- Add vanilla and protein powder and stir well to combine.
- Now add peanuts and cherries and fold gently but quickly.
- Transfer batter to a prepared pan and freeze until it sets.
- Slice into bars upon setting and enjoy.

e) **No-Bake Almond Fudge**

Ingredients:

- Oats, 1 cup, ground into flour
- Honey, ½ cup
- Quick oats, ½ cup
- Almond butter, ½ cup
- Vanilla extract, 1 teaspoon
- Vanilla protein powder, ½ cup
- Chocolate chips, 3 tablespoons Crispy rice cereal, ½ cup

Method:

- Spray a loaf pan with cooking spray and keep aside. Combine rice cereal with oats flour and quick oats. Keep aside.
- Melt almond butter with honey in a pan then add vanilla.
- Transfer this mixture to the dry ingredients bowl and mix well.
- Transfer to prepared pan and even out using a spatula.
- Refrigerate for 30 minutes or until firm.
- Meanwhile melt chocolate.
- Remove the mixture from pan and drizzle melted chocolate on top. Refrigerate again until the chocolate sets then slice into bars of your desired size.

f) Red Velvet Fudge ProteinBars

Ingredients:

a) Roasted beets puree, 185 g
b) Vanilla bean paste, 1 teaspoon
c) Unsweetened soy milk, ½ cup
d) Nut butter, 128 g
e) Pink Himalayan salt, 1/8 teaspoon
f) Extract (butter), 2 teaspoons
g) Raw stevia, ¾ cup
h) Oat flour, 80 g
i) Protein powder, 210 g

Method:

a) Melt butter in a saucepan and add oats flour, protein powder, beets puree, vanilla, extract, salt and stevia. Stir until combined.
b) Now add soy milk and stir until well incorporated.
c) Transfer the mixture to a pan and refrigerate for 25 minutes.
d) When the mixture is firm, slice into 6 bars and enjoy.

g) Fudge Munchies

Servings: 6-8

Ingredients:

- 1/2 Cup butter
- 1/2 Cup Almond Butter
- 1/8 to 1/4 cup Honey
- 1/2 of a Banana, Mashed
- 1 tsp. Vanilla Extract
- any kind of nut butter
- 1/8 Cup Dried Fruit
- 1/8 Cup Chocolate Chips

Directions:

a) In a blender or food processer, add in all the ingredients. Blend for several minutes until smooth. 2. Pour the batter into a loaf pan with the lining of baking paper.
b) For larger chunks, use a mini loaf pan or double the recipe. Refrigerate or freeze until firm. Cut into 8 equal squares.

c) 

a) Frosted Mocha Brownies

- 1 c. sugar
- 1/2 c. butter, softened
- 1/3 c. baking cocoa
- 1 t. instant coffee granules
- 2 eggs, beaten
- 1 t. vanilla extract
- 2/3 c. all-purpose flour
- 1/2 t. baking powder
- 1/4 t. salt
- 1/2 c. chopped walnuts

- Combine sugar, butter, cocoa and coffee granules in a saucepan. Cook and stir over medium heat until butter is melted. Remove from heat; cool for 5 minutes. Add eggs and vanilla; stir until just combined.
- Blend in flour, baking powder and salt; fold in nuts. Spread batter in a greased 9"x9" baking pan. Bake at 350 degrees for 25 minutes, or until set.
- Cool in pan on a wire rack. Spread Mocha Frosting over cooled brownies; slice into bars. Makes one dozen.

b) Pecan butter chia seed blondies

INGREDIENTS

- 2 1/4 cups Pecans, roasted
- 1/2 cup Chia Seeds
- 1/4 cup Butter, melted
- 1/4 cup Erythritol, powdered
- tbsp. SF Torani Salted

Caramel

a) drops Liquid Stevia
b) large Eggs
c) 1 tsp. Baking Powder
d) 3 tbsp. Heavy Cream
e) 1 pinch Salt

DIRECTIONS

- Preheat oven to 350F. Measure out 2 1/4 cup pecans
- Grind 1/2 cup whole chia seeds in a spice grinder until a meal forms.
- Remove chia meal and place in a bowl. Next, grind 1/4 cup Erythritol in a spice grinder until powdered. Set in the same bowl as the chia meal.
- Place 2/3 of roasted pecans in food processor.
- Process nuts, scraping sides down as needed, until smooth nut butter is formed.
- Add 3 large eggs, 10 drops liquid stevia, 3 tbsp. SF Salted Caramel Torani Syrup, and a pinch of salt to the chia mixture. Mix this together well.
- Add pecan butter to the batter and mix again.
- Using a rolling pin, smash the rest of the roasted pecans into chunks inside of a plastic bag.

- Add crushed pecans and 1/4 cup melted butter into the batter.
- Mix batter well, and then add 3 tbsp. Heavy cream and 1 tsp. Baking Powder. Mix everything together well.
- Measure out the batter into a 9×9 tray and smooth out.
- Bake for 20 minutes or until desired consistency.
- Let cool for about 10 minutes. Slice off the edges of the brownie to create a uniform square. This is what I call "the bakers treat" – yep, you guessed it!
- Snack on those bad boys while you get them ready to serve to everyone else. The so-called "best part" of the brownie are the edges, and that's why you deserve to have all of it.
- Serve up and eat to your hearts (or rather macros) content!

c) Apple Brownies

a) 1/2 c. butter, softened
b) 1 c. sugar
c) 1 t. vanilla extract
d) 1 egg, beaten
e) 1-1/2 c. all-purpose flour
f) 1/2 t. baking soda

- Preheat oven to 350 degrees F (175 degrees C). Grease a 9x9 inch baking dish.
- In a large bowl, beat together the melted butter, sugar, and egg until fluffy. Fold in the apples and walnuts. In a separate bowl, sift together the flour, salt, baking powder, baking soda, and cinnamon.
- Stir the flour mixture into the wet mixture until just blended. Spread the batter evenly in the prepared baking dish.
- Bake 35 minutes in the preheated oven, or until a toothpick inserted in the center comes out clean.

d) Peppermint Bark Brownies

- 20-oz. pkg. fudge brownie mix
- 12-oz. pkg. white chocolate chips
- 2 t. margarine
- 1-1/2 c. candy canes, crushed

1 Prepare and bake brownie mix according to package directions, using a greased 13"x9" baking pan. After baking, cool completely in pan.
2 In a saucepan over very low heat, melt chocolate chips and margarine, stirring constantly with a rubber spatula. Spread mixture over brownies; sprinkle with crushed candy.
3 Let stand for about 30 minutes before cutting into squares. Makes 2 dozen.

e) **Keto peanut butter fudge bars**

INGREDIENTS

The Crust

a) 1 cup Almond Flour
b) 1/4 cup Butter, melted
c) 1/2 tsp. Cinnamon
d) 1 tbsp. Erythritol
e) Pinch of Salt

The Fudge

a) 1/4 cup Heavy Cream
b) 1/4 cup Butter, melted
c) 1/2 cup Peanut Butter
d) 1/4 cup Erythritol
e) 1/2 tsp. Vanilla Extract
f) 1/8 tsp. Xanthan Gum

The Toppings

g) 1/3 cup Lily's Chocolate, Chopped

DIRECTIONS

- Preheat the oven to 400°F. Melt 1/2 cup butter. Half will be for the crust and half for the fudge. Combine the almond flour and half the melted butter.
- Add erythritol and cinnamon, and then mix together. If you're using unsalted butter, add a pinch of salt to bring out more flavors.
- Mix until even throughout and press into the bottom of a baking dish lined with parchment paper. Bake the crust for 10 minutes or until edges are golden brown. Take it out and let it cool.
- For the filling, combine all the fudge ingredients in a small blender or food processor and blend. You can use an electric hand mixer and bowl as well.
- Make sure to scrape down the sides and get all the ingredients well combined.
- After the crust is cooled, spread the fudge layer gently all the way up to the sides of the baking dish. Use a spatula to even out the top as best you can.
- Just before chilling, top your bars off with some chopped chocolate. This can be in the form of sugar-free chocolate chips, sugar-free dark chocolate or just good old dark chocolate. I used Lily's Stevia Sweetened chocolate.
- Refrigerate overnight or freeze if you want it soon.
- When cooled, remove the bars by pulling the parchment paper out. Cu in 8-10 bars and serve! These peanut butter fudge bars should be enjoyed chilled! If you take them to go, make sure to carry them in an insulated lunch bag to keep them firm.

CHOCOLATE

f) **Favorite Zucchini Brownies**

h) 1/4 c. butter, melted
i) 1 c. sPeanut Butter Brownies
j) 1 egg, beaten
k) 1 t. vanilla extract
l) 1 c. all-purpose flour
m) 1 t. baking powder
n) 1/2 t. baking soda
o) 1 T. water
p) 1/2 t. salt
q) 2-1/2 T. baking cocoa
r) 1/2 c. chopped walnuts
s) 3/4 c. zucchini, shredded
t) 1/2 c. semi-sweet chocolate chips

- In a large bowl, blend together all ingredients except chocolate chips.
- Spread batter in a greased 8"x8" baking pan; sprinkle batter with chocolate chips.
- Bake at 350 degrees for 35 minutes. Cool before cutting into bars. Makes one dozen.

g) Malt Chocolate Brownies

- 12-oz. pkg. milk chocolate chips
- 1/2 c. butter, softened
- 3/4 c. sugar
- 1 t. vanilla extract
- 3 eggs, beaten
- 1-3/4 c. all-purpose flour
- 1/2 c. malted milk powder
- 1/2 t. salt
- 1 c. malted milk balls, coarsely chopped

1. Melt chocolate chips and butter in a saucepan over low heat, stirring frequently. Remove from heat; allow to cool slightly.
2. Blend in remaining ingredients except malted milk balls in the order given.
3. Spread batter in a greased 13"x9" baking pan. Sprinkle with malted milk balls; bake at 350 degrees for 30 to 35 minutes. Cool. Cut into bars. Makes 2 dozen.

h) German Chocolate Brownies

- 14-oz. pkg. caramels, unwrapped
- 1/3 c. evaporated milk
- 18-1/4 oz. pkg. German chocolate cake mix
- 1 c. chopped nuts
- 3/4 c. butter, melted
- 1 to 2 c. semi-sweet chocolate chips

1. Melt caramels with evaporated milk in a double boiler. In a bowl, combine dry cake mix, nuts and butter; stir until mixture comes together. Press half the batter into a greased and floured 13"x9" baking pan.
2. Bake at 350 degrees for 6 minutes. Remove from oven; sprinkle with chocolate chips and drizzle with caramel mixture. Spoon remaining batter over top.
3. Bake at 350 degrees for 15 to 18 minutes longer. Cool; cut into bars. Makes 1-1/2 dozen.

16. Matcha Green Tea Fudge

Ingredients:

- Roasted almond butter, 85 g
- Oat flour, 60 g
- Unsweetened vanilla almond milk, 1 cup
- Protein powder, 168 g
- Dark chocolate, 4 oz. melted
- Matcha green tea powder, 4 teaspoons
- Stevia extract, 1 teaspoon
- Lemon, 10 drops

Method:

1. Melt butter in a saucepan and add oats flour, tea powder, protein powder, lemon drops and stevia. Mix well.
2. Now pour milk and stir constantly until well combined.
3. Transfer the mixture to a loaf pan and refrigerate until set.
4. Drizzle melted chocolate on top and refrigerate again until the chocolate is firm.
5. Slice into 5 bars and enjoy.

17. Gingerbread Brownies

- 1-1/2 c. all-purpose flour
- 1 c. sugar
- 1/2 t. baking soda
- 1/4 c. baking cocoa
- 1 t. ground ginger
- 1 t. cinnamon
- 1/2 t. ground cloves
- 1/4 c. butter, melted and slightly cooled
- 1/3 c. molasses
- 2 eggs, beaten
- Garnish: powdered sugar

1. In a large bowl, combine flour, sugar, baking soda, cocoa and spices. In a separate bowl, combine butter, molasses and eggs. Add butter mixture to flour mixture, stirring until just combined.
2. Spread batter in a greased 13"x9" baking pan. Bake at 350 degrees for 20 minutes, or until a toothpick tests clean when inserted into center.
3. Cool in pan on a wire rack. Sprinkle with powdered sugar. Cut into squares. Makes 2 dozen.

18. Honey Chocolate Brownies

Ingredients:

- 1 cup melted butter or oil
- ½ cup melted unsweetened chocolate or cocoa powder
- 4 eggs
- 1 cup honey
- 2 teaspoons vanilla
- 2 cups unbleached white flour
- 2 teaspoons baking powder
- ½ teaspoon sea salt
- 1 cup raisin s
- 1 cup chopped nuts

Directions:

- Preheat oven to 350 degrees F.
- Whip the butter, chocolate, carob or cocoa and honey together until smooth. Add eggs and vanilla; mix well.
- Add the dry ingredients, stir until dampened. Add the raisins and nuts and mix thoroughly.
- Pour batter into a greased 9x13 inch baking pan. Bake for 45 minutes or until done.
- Cut into 24 equal pieces (approximately 2‖ x 2‖), each serving has 2 teaspoons of butter = high dose, or cut into 48 pieces (about 2‖ x 1‖) = medium dose.

19. Mint brownies

Ingredients:

- 1 cup butter
- 6 ounces unsweetened chocolate
- 2 cups sugar
- 1 teaspoon baking powder
- 1½ teaspoons vanilla
- ½ teaspoon salt
- 1½ cups flou r
- 1 cup walnuts or pecans, finely ground
- 1 1/2 ounces bag Hershey's mint chocolate chips
- 4 eggs

Directions:

- Preheat oven.
- In a medium saucepan, melt butter and unsweetened chocolate over low heat, stirring constantly. Remove from heat and let cool.
- Grease 9×13 inch pan and set aside. Stir sugar into cooled chocolate mixture in saucepan. Beat eggs, and add slowly to chocolate mixture. Stir in vanilla.
- In a bowl, stir together the flour, baking soda and salt.
- Add flour mixture to chocolate mixture until combined. Stir in nuts and mint chocolate chips. Spread the batter in the prepared pan.
- Bake for 30 minutes. Cool on wire rack before storing.

20. Pecan Brownies

Ingredients:

a) 1 cup butter
b) 2/3 cup chocolate
c) 1 teaspoon vanilla extract
d) Orange zest (optional)
e) 5egg whites
f) 4 egg yolk s
g) 3/4 cup sugar
h) 1/3 cup flour
i) 1 tablespoon cocoa powder
j) 1/2 cup crushed pecan nuts

Directions:

- Preheat oven to 220 degrees F.
- Use a double boiler by placing a bowl on top of a pot with water over medium high heat.
- Add your chocolate, butter, vanilla extract and orange zest to the empty bowl and mix to incorporate.
- Take the bowl off the heat and set aside. (You will not need any heat anymore from this point on.)
- Place your egg whites in a separate bowl.
- Beat egg whites until you form stiff white peaks, using an electric mixer or a whisk; set aside.
- Add your egg yolks to another separate bowl and add sugar. Mix to incorporate.
- Add your chocolate mixture to the egg-yolk mixture and slowly incorporate both using a spatula.
- Once incorporated, sift in your flour, cocoa powder and add your pecan nuts.
- Now add your fluffy white egg whites to the mixture, and incorporate everything together using a spatula. Line a baking pan with parchment paper and add your finished mixture to it.
- Now bake for 60 minutes, and your brownies will be ready.

21. Mint brownies with toffee sauce

INGREDIENTS

Brownies

a) 1 cup (230g) unsalted butter
b) 2 ounces semi-sweet chocolate, coarsely chopped
c) 1 and 1/2 cups (300g) granulated sugar
d) 1/2 cup (100g) packed light brown sugar
e) 2 large eggs, at room temperature
f) 2 teaspoons pure vanilla extract
g) 1/2 teaspoon salt
h) 1/2 cup + 3 Tablespoons (85g) all-purpose flour (spoon & leveled)
i) 1/4 cup (21g) natural unsweetened cocoa powder

Mint Frosting Layer

- 1/2 cup (115g) unsalted butter, softened to room temperature
- 2 cups (240g) confectioners' sugar
- 2 Tablespoons (30ml) milk
- 1 and 1/4 teaspoons peppermint extract*
- optional: 1 drop liquid or gel green food coloring

Chocolate Layer

- 1/2 cup (115g) unsalted butter
- 1 heaping cup (around 200g) semi-sweet chocolate chips

Salted toffee sauce

1. 7 TBSP. butter
2. 9 TBSP. unsalted butter
3. 1 cup heavy cream
4. 1 cup dark brown sugar, firmly packed
5. ½ tsp. salt

Instructions

For the brownies:

1. Melt the butter and chopped chocolate in a medium saucepan on medium heat, stirring constantly, about 5 minutes. Or melt in a medium microwave safe bowl in 20 second increments, stirring after each, in the microwave. Remove from the heat, pour into a large mixing bowl, and allow to slightly cool for 10 minutes.
2. Adjust the oven rack to the lower third position and preheat oven to 350°F (177°C). Line the bottom and sides of a 9×13 baking pan* with aluminum foil or parchment paper, leaving an overhang on all sides. Set aside.
3. Whisk the granulated and brown sugars into the cooled chocolate/butter mixture. Add the eggs, one at a time, whisking until smooth after each addition. Whisk in the vanilla. Gently fold in the salt, flour, and cocoa powder. Pour batter into the prepared baking pan and bake for 35-36 minutes or until the brownies begin to pull away from the edges of the pan.
4. Once completely cooled, lift the foil out of the pan using the overhang on the sides. Place the whole thing on a baking sheet as you make the frosting. Do not cut into squares yet.

For the mint frosting layer:

- In a medium bowl using a handheld or stand mixer fitted with a paddle attachment, beat the butter on medium speed until smooth and creamy, about 2 minutes. Add the confectioners' sugar and milk. Beat for 2 minutes on low speed, then increase to high speed and beat for 1 additional minute. Add the peppermint extract and food coloring (if using) and beat on high for 1 full minute. Taste and add a drop or two more peppermint extract if desired.
- Frost cooled brownies that you placed on the baking sheet, and place the baking sheet in the refrigerator. This allows the frosting to "set" on top of the brownies which makes spreading the chocolate layer easy. Keep in the refrigerator for at least 1 hour and up to 4 hours.

For the chocolate layer:

a) Melt the butter and chocolate chips in a medium saucepan on medium heat, stirring constantly, about 5 minutes. Or melt in a medium microwave safe bowl in 20 second increments, stirring after each, in the microwave. Once melted and smooth, pour over mint layer.
b) Gently spread with a knife or offset spatula. Place the brownies that are still on the baking sheet, in the refrigerator and chill for 1 hour (and up to 4 hours or even overnight) to set the chocolate.
c) Once chilled, remove from the refrigerator and cut into squares. For neat cutting, make very quick cuts, using a very sharp large knife, and wiping the knife off with a paper towel between each cut. Brownies are OK at room temperature for a few hours. Cover tightly and keep leftovers in the refrigerator for up to 5 days.

For the Toffee Sauce:

- In a medium saucepan over medium-low heat, combine butter, unsalted butter, heavy cream, dark brown sugar, and salt. Bring to a simmer, stirring frequently.
- Continue to simmer for 10 minutes until sauce begins to reduce in size and thicken. Remove from heat. Allow sauce to cool slightly before serving.

22. Chocolate & Nutmeg Brownies

Ingredients:

1. 1/4 pound butter
2. 1/4 pound dark chocolate
3. 1 cup of white sugar
4. 4 regular eggs
5. 1/2 cup plain flour
6. Nutmeg
7. Cinnamon
8. 2 tablespoons of vanilla

Directions

- Preheat your oven to 350 degrees F.
- Melt the butter over a low heat, then add the chocolate (in cubes is quickest) and melt that in with the already melted butter; stir regularly so that it becomes chocolate butter!
- As soon as the chocolate has melted entirely, add the cinnamon, nutmeg and the white sugar; stir and simmer for a few minutes.
- Add the eggs, one at a time, beating them so that the yolk breaks up. Continue to stir the mixture on a low heat until it is completely smooth.
- Add theflour and finely ground cannabis to the mix. If you like nuts, then you can add a quarter of a cup of your favorite nut if you wish. Stir it well; if it is difficult to stir, then add a small dash of milk.
- Pour your mixture into a greased 9x13 inch pan if you don‘t have one then a smaller one is OK – it just means a thicker brownie and possibly a little longer in the oven.
- Bake your mixture for 20-25 minutes, sometimes a little longer is required.
- Once it looks and feels like a giant brownie, cut it into around 20 square. It doesn‘t matter how many squares, of course.
- Dosage: Wait an hour and see how you feel. Then eat more as required! These brownies taste delicious and it is difficult to

resist eating them, but you don‘t want to eat too many and then whitey!

23. Peanut Butter Swirl Brownie

Ingredients:

- 2 tablespoons cannabutter, softened
- 2 tablespoons sugar
- 1 1/2 tablespoons brown sugar
- 1 tablespoon cocoa powder
- 1 egg yolk
- 3 tablespoons flour
- Pinch of salt
- Splash of vanilla
- 1 tablespoon creamy peanut butter

Directions:

1. Mix the cannabutter, sugar, brown sugar, vanilla and egg yolk until smooth .
2. Stir in the salt and flour until well combined. Stir chocolate chips in last.
3. Pour into a ramekin or mug, then dot the top with peanut butter.
4. Swirl lightly with a butter knife.
5. 5.75 seconds in the microwave until just done.

24. Pumpkin Brownies

Ingredients:

1. 2/3 cup packed brown sugar
2. 1/2 cup canned pumpkin
3. 1 whole egg
4. 2 egg whites
5. 1/4 cup cannabutter
6. 1 cup all-purpose flour
7. 1 teaspoon baking powder
8. 1 teaspoon unsweetened cocoa powder
9. 1/2 teaspoon ground cinnamon
10. 1/2 teaspoon ground allspice
11. 1/4 teaspoon salt
12. 1/4 teaspoon ground nutme g
13. 1/3 cup miniature semisweet chocolate pieces

Directions:

- Preheat oven to 350 degrees F.
- In a large mixing bowl, combine brown sugar, pumpkin, the whole egg, egg whites and oil.
- Beat with an electric mixer on medium speed until blended.
- Add flour, baking powder, cocoa powder, cinnamon, allspice, salt and nutmeg
- Beat on low speed until smooth. Stir in semisweet chocolate pieces.
- Spray an 11×7 inch baking pan with nonstick coating.
- Pour batter into pan. Spread evenly.
- Bake 15 to 20 minutes or until a toothpick inserted near the center comes out clean.

BARKS, PRETZELS & NOUGATINES

25. Peppermint Buddha Bark

Ingredients:

1. 12 ounces white chocolate
2. 6 ounces semisweet chocolate
3. 4 tablespoons coconut oil
4. ½ teaspoon peppermint extract
5. 3 candy canes (crushed)

Directions

- Line a 9×9 inch baking pan with some parchment paper or aluminum foil, making sure to wrap the foil over the sides of the pan, and smooth out any wrinkles as you go. This step will ensure a quick clean upand will also allow for the peppermint bark to easily pop off the pan when it comes time to break it into individual pieces.
- Melt together the semisweet chocolate chips and the white chocolate chips. To do this, create a double boiler using a heat-safe bowl and a saucepan filled with water. Choose a bowl that fits snugly over the top of the saucepan (Do not use a bowl that sits precariously on top of the pot). You also want to ensure that the bottom of the bowl does not touch the water or you risk burning the chocolate.
- As a aside, this recipe uses 3 layers of chocolate for the bark (white, semisweet, white). Feel free to switch up the quantities of the chocolate and reverse the layering (semisweet, white, semisweet) if you so please!
- Bring the water in the saucepan to a simmer, and place the heat-safe bowl containing your white chocolate chips over the sauce pan.
- Melt the white chocolate chips until they‘re smooth
- Add in 4 tablespoons of cannabis-infused coconut oil and the ½ teaspoon of peppermint extract.
- Stir until both oils have fully dissolved into the white chocolate. Aside from medicating the dish, the coconut oil will also create a nice shine in the bark and allow it to have a good —snap‖ when breaking up the pieces.

- Once themelted white chocolate is smooth again, pour half of it into the prepped pan. Tilt the pan after you pour in half of the melted white chocolate to ensure an even coating/first layer.
- Place the pan in the refrigerator and allow the first layer of chocolate to harden completely, roughly 30 minutes or so.
- While your first layer of bark is setting, repeat the above steps in order to prepare a second double boiler for your semi-sweet chocolate chips.
- Once your semisweet chocolate chips are completely melted, remove the bowl from the double boiler.
- Take the pan containing the first layer of white chocolate from the refrigerator and proceed to pour the entire bowl of melted semisweet chocolate chips over the first layer. It is extremely important that the

  initial layer of white chocolate is completely hardened, as introducing the second layer will cause them to mix if this is not the case
- Spread the second layer of semisweet chocolate chips evenly throughout the pan using a spatula or baker's knife.
- Place the pan back into the refrigerator as you wait for the second layer of chocolate to set, again roughly 30 minutes or so.
- When the second layer of chocolate has set, add the third and final layer of white chocolate on top of the semisweet layer. Spread this third layer evenly with a spatula.
- Place the candy canes into a Ziploc bag and proceed to crush them into tiny pieces using the back of a ladle or a rolling pin.
- Sprinkle the crushed candy canes on top of the third and final layer of white chocolate covering the entire surface, and then place the pan back into the refrigerator until the bark is completely set (30 minutes to 1 hour).
- When ready to eat, remove the bark from the refrigerator and pull up on the sides of the aluminum foil – the bark should lift right out of the pan!
- Break the bark into individual pieces, and either package them up to give as a gift, or serve them to your guests immediately!

26. Chocolate bark with candied pecans

Ingredients:

a) 2 TBSP. butter
b) 1 cup pecan halves
c) 2 TBSP. light or dark brown sugar, firmly packed
d) 2 cups dark chocolate chips
e) 2 TBSP. crystallized ginger

Directions

a) In a small saucepan over low heat, heat butter for 2 to 3 minutes or until fully melted. Add pecan halves and stir for 3 to 5 minutes until fragrant and nutty. Mix in light brown sugar, stirring constantly, for about 1 minute or until pecans are coated evenly and have begun to caramelize. Remove from heat.
b) Spread caramelized pecans on parchment paper and allow cooling. Roughly chop pecans and set aside.
c) In a double boiler over medium heat, stir dark chocolate chips for 5 to 7 minutes or until completely melted.
d) On a baking sheet lined with parchment paper, spread melted chocolate.
e) Sprinkle caramelized pecans and crystallized ginger evenly on top. Set aside for 1 to 2 hours or until chocolate has set. Cut or break bark into 6 even pieces.
f) Storage: Keep covered in an airtight container in the refrigerator for up to 6 weeks or in the freezer for up to 6 months.

a) **Pecan butter chia seed blondies**

INGREDIENTS

- 2 1/4 cups Pecans, roasted
- 1/2 cup Chia Seeds
- 1/4 cup Butter, melted
- 1/4 cup Erythritol, powdered
- 3 tbsp. SF Torani Salted Caramel
- drops Liquid Stevia
- 3 large Eggs
- 1 tsp. Baking Powder
- 3 tbsp. Heavy Cream
- 1 pinch Salt

DIRECTIONS

a) Preheat oven to 350F. Measure out 2 1/4 cup pecans and bake for about 10 minutes. Once you can smell a nutty aroma, remove nuts

b) Grind 1/2 cup whole chia seeds in a spice grinder until a meal forms.

c) Remove chia meal and place in a bowl. Next, grind 1/4 cup Erythritol in a spice grinder until powdered. Set in the same bowl as the chia meal.

d) Place 2/3 of roasted pecans in food processor.

e) Process nuts, scraping sides down as needed, until smooth nut butter is formed.

f) Add 3 large eggs, 10 drops liquid stevia, 3 tbsp. SF Salted Caramel Torani Syrup, and a pinch of salt to the chia mixture. Mix this together well.

g) Add pecan butter to the batter and mix again.

h) Using a rolling pin, smash the rest of the roasted pecans into chunks inside of a plastic bag.

i) Add crushed pecans and 1/4 cup melted butter into the batter.

j) Mix batter well, and then add 3 tbsp. Heavy cream and 1 tsp. Baking Powder. Mix everything together well.
k) Measure out the batter into a 9×9 tray and smooth out.
l) Bake for 20 minutes or until desired consistency.
m) Let cool for about 10 minutes. Slice off the edges of the brownie to create a uniform square. This is what I call "the bakers treat" – yep, you guessed it!
n) Snack on those bad boys while you get them ready to serve to everyone else. The so-called "best part" of the brownie are the edges, and that's why you deserve to have all of it.
o) Serve up and eat to your hearts (or rather macros) content!

28. Chocolate-dipped dried mango

Ingredients:

a) 1 cup dark chocolate chips
b) 2 TBSP. coconut oil
c) 12 large pieces unsweetened dried mango
d) 6 TBSP. shredded coconut (optional)

Directions

- Line a baking sheet with parchment paper and set aside. In a double boiler over medium heat, combine dark chocolate chips and coconut oil.
- Stir for 5 to 7 minutes or until chocolate is fully melted and thoroughly combined with coconut oil. Remove from heat.
- With a fork or your hands, dip each mango piece into melted chocolate and let any excess drip back into the bowl. Place dipped mango pieces on the prepared baking sheet.
- Sprinkle shredded coconut (if using) over dipped mango pieces. Refrigerate for 30 minutes or until chocolate is set.
- Storage: Keep covered in an airtight container in the refrigerator for up to 6 weeks or in the freezer for up to 6 months.

29. Pretzel rods with white chocolate

Ingredients:

- ¼ cup toffee bits
- 1 cup white chocolate melts
- 2 TBSP. butter
- 6 pretzel rods

Directions

- Line a baking sheet with parchment paper and set aside. Pour toffee bits onto a shallow plate near the baking sheet.
- In a double boiler over medium heat, combine white chocolate melts and butter, stirring occasionally, for 5 to 7 minutes until white chocolate is completely melted.
- Dip ¾ of each pretzel rod into melted white chocolate, allowing any excess chocolate to drip back into the pot.
- Roll each pretzel rod in toffee bits and place on the prepared baking sheet. Allow to set for at least 30 minutes.

- Storage: Keep in an airtight container in the refrigerator for up to 1 month.

30. Chocolate-dipped nougatine

Ingredients:

a) ¾ cup granulated sugar
b) ⅓ cup light corn syrup
c) ¼ cup chopped pistachios
d) ¾ cup sliced almonds
e) 2 TBSP. butter
f) 1 cup dark chocolate chips

Directions

a) Line a baking sheet with parchment paper and set aside. In a medium saucepan over medium heat, stir sugar and light corn syrup for 5 to 7 minutes until mixture is melted and starting to caramelize.
b) Mix in pistachios, almonds, and butter, and stir for 2 to 3 minutes to lightly toast almonds. (Don't boil.)
c) Transfer nougatine mixture onto the prepared baking sheet and top with an additional sheet of parchment paper. Spread evenly with a rolling pin until about ½ inch (1.25cm) thick. Cut into 12 pieces.
d) In a double boiler over medium heat, heat dark chocolate chips for 5 to 7 minutes or until melted.
e) Dip nougatine pieces into melted chocolate, covering just half of nougatine, and return to the parchment-lined baking sheet. Allow chocolate to set for at least 1 hour.
f) Storage: Keep in an airtight container for up to 1 week.

DESSERT TRUFFLES & BALLS

31. Peanut Butter Balls

Items Needed:

- Mixing bowl
- Double boiler
- Tray
- Wax paper
- Toothpicks

Ingredients:

- 1 1/2 cups peanut butter
- 1 cup cannabutter (hardened)
- 4 cups confectioners' suga r
- 1 1/3 cups Graham cracker crumbs
- 2 cups semisweet chocolate chips
- 1 tablespoon shortening

Directions:

a) Place the peanut butter and the cannabutter in a large mixing bowl. Slowly blend in the confectioners'sugar making sure that it does not get messy. Add Graham cracker crumbs and mix till consistency becomes solid enough to shape into balls.
b) Make one-inch diameter balls.
c) Melt the chocolate chips and shortening in a double bottomed boiler. Prick a toothpick into each ball, and then dip them one by one in the chocolate mixture.
d) Place the chocolate wrapped balls on wax paper on a tray. Place in the freezer for about 30 minutes until the balls are all solid.

32. Ancho chile truffles

Ingredients:

a) ⅔ cup heavy cream
b) 5 TBSP. butter
c) 3 tsp. ancho chile powder
d) 2 tsp. ground cinnamon
e) Dash salt
f) ½ lb. (225g) bittersweet chocolate, chopped
g) 1 tsp. cocoa powder

Directions

1. Line a 9×13-inch (23×33cm) baking pan with parchment paper and set aside. In a medium saucepan over medium-low heat, combine heavy cream, 3 tablespoons butter, 2 teaspoons ancho chile powder, cinnamon, and salt. Bring mixture to a boil, cover, and remove from heat. Let stand for 2 hours.
2. Return the saucepan to medium-low heat. Once it reaches a simmer, remove from heat and add bittersweet chocolate and remaining 2 tablespoons butter. Stir for 2 to 3 minutes or until chocolate is melted and mixture is smooth. Pour into the prepared baking pan and chill in the refrigerator for 4 hours.
3. Using a spoon and your hands, form mixture into 16 1-inch (2.5cm) balls. Place balls on a clean parchment paper–lined baking sheet and chill in the refrigerator for 30 minutes.
4. In a small bowl, combine remaining 1 teaspoon ancho chile powder and cocoa powder. Roll balls in powder and place back on the parchment paper.
5. Storage: Enjoy the same day at room temperature or keep in an airtight container in the refrigerator for up to 1 week.

33. Chocolate Truffles

Preparation Time: 15-20 minutes
Cooking Time: 0 minutes
Servings: 10-12

Ingredients:

- ½ cup butter softened
- ½cup powdered sugar
- ¼cup unsweetened cocoa powder
- ½cup almond flour
- Large pinch salt
- Dash almond extract
- Dash vanilla extract
- 24whole almonds, toasted in butter and Salt
- 1cup unsweetened shredded coconut

Directions:

- Line a baking sheet with parchment paper. In a bowl, put all the prepared ingredients except the whole almonds and coconut and mix gently until the mixture is fairly smooth.
- Roll teaspoons of the mixture between your palms into balls. (Work quickly, as the butter gets very soft quickly. Refrigerate for a few minutes if the mixture gets too soft.)
- If using the toasted almonds, tuck one into the center of each and roll again quickly to smooth things over.
- Place the coconut in a bowl and roll the balls in the coconut until coated. Place on the baking sheet and refrigerate to firm up. Store the munchies in a glass container in the fridge.

34. Chocolate Covered Cherries

Preparation Time: 1 ½ hr.
Cooking Time: 5 minutes
Servings: 12

Ingredients:

- 24 cherries with stems (remove the pits or use dried ones)
- 1 cup milk chocolate chips
- 1 cup dark chocolate chips
- ¼ cup of coconut oil

Directions:

a) In a microwave-safe bowl, heat dark chocolate chips, milk chocolate chips and coconut oil.
b) Heat the mix for 20-seconds intervals and stir by turns until it has finally melted.
c) Ensure the chocolate is not too hot. Cover the cherries with chocolate, and let the excess chocolate drip. Set the cherries onto a wax-lined paper.
d) Once all the cherries are done, transfer them into the refrigerator for 1-hour
e) Double coat the cherries if you want (transfer into the refrigerator again) Enjoy!

35. Neapolitan fudge

INGREDIENTS

a) ½ cup butter softened
b) 1/2 cup Coconut Oil
c) 1/2 cup Sour Cream
d) 1/2 cup Cream Cheese
e) 2 tbsp. Erythritol
f) 25 drops Liquid Stevia
g) 2 tbsp. Cocoa Powder
h) 1 tsp. Vanilla Extract
i) 2 medium Strawberries

DIRECTIONS

9. In a bowl, combine butter, coconut oil, sour cream, cream cheese, erythritol, and liquid stevia.
10. Using an immersion blender, blend together the ingredients into a smooth mixture.
11. Divide the mixture into 3 different bowls. Add cocoa powder to one bowl, strawberries to another bowl, and vanilla to the last bowl.
12. Mix together all of the ingredients again using an immersion blender. Separate the chocolate mixture into a container with a spout.
13. Pour chocolate mixture into fat bomb mold. Place in freezer for 30 minutes, then repeat with the vanilla mixture.
14. Freeze vanilla mixture for 30 minutes, and then repeat process with strawberry mixture. Freeze again for at least 1 hour.
15. Once they're completely frozen, remove from the fat bomb molds.

36. Cheesy Broccoli balls

INGREDIENTS

The Fritters

- 250 g melted butter
- 3/4 cup Almond Flour
- 1/4 cup + 3 tbsp. Flaxseed Meal
- oz. Fresh Broccoli
- oz. Mozzarella Cheese
- 2 large Eggs
- 2 tsp. Baking Powder
- Salt and Pepper to Taste

DIRECTIONS

- Add broccoli to a food processor and pulse until the broccoli is broken down into small pieces. You want it to be well processed.
- Mix together the cheese, almond flour, butter, flaxseed mcal and baking powder with the broccoli. If you want to add any extra seasonings (salt and pepper), do it at this point.
- Add the 2 eggs and mix together well until everything is incorporated.
- Roll the batter into balls and then coat with flaxseed meal.
- Continue doing this with all of the batter and set aside on paper towels.
- Heat your deep fat fryer to 375F. I use this deep fat fryer. Once ready, lay broccoli and cheese fritters inside the basket, not overcrowding it.
- Fry the fritters until golden brown, about 3-5 minutes. Once done, lay on paper towels to drain excess grease and season to your tastes.
- Feel free to make a zesty dill and lemon mayonnaise for a dip. Enjoy

37. Chocolate-Dipped Cherries

Ingredients:

- 1 cup dark chocolate chips
- 1 cup milk chocolate chips
- ¼ cup coconut oil
- 24 cherries with stems (washed and dried; if you use fresh cherries, remember to remove the pit!)

Directions:

- Heat milk chocolate chips, dark chocolate chips and coconut oil in a microwave safe bowl. Remove and stir every 20 seconds until melted. Chocolate should be warm but not hot.
- Dip dry cherries by the stems in chocolate, one at a time, allowing excess chocolate to drip back into bowl.
- Set cherries on a wax paper-lined plate to dry. Repeat until all cherries are coated. Save extra chocolate on the side
- Chill cherries in the refrigerator for 1 hour.
- Warm the chocolate sauce back up and remove cherries from the refrigerator.
- Dip each cherry in the chocolate sauce for a second time. Return cherries to the refrigerator to chill for 1 hour before

serving.

38. Mint Patties

Ingredients:

- ½ cup of light corn syrup
- 2 teaspoon of peppermint extract
- ½ cup of softened butter
- 2 drops of food coloring (optional)
- 9 cups of sifted powdered sugar (about 2 pounds)

Directions:

a) Use a mixing bowl to mix the corn syrup, peppermint extract, and slightly melted Baked Butter or margarine. Then add the sugar, a little bit at a time, and incorporate it into the mix. Add the amount of food coloring to achieve your desired color and blend well.

b) Roll this mixture into small balls. Place them a few inches apart from each other on a baking sheet that has been lined with wax paper. Use a fork to make each one flat.

c) Let the mint patties set in the refrigerator for several hours. Remove the patties from the refrigerator and let stand at room temperature for several days to dry out.

d) After a few days, when the patties are dried out, transfer them to a container with an airtight lid and store them in the refrigerator.

39. Coconut Marshmallow Balls

Ingredients:

- 2 ounces butter
- 2 tablespoons cocoa
- 3 tablespoons condensed milk
- 2 ounce brown sugar
- 1/8 ounce finely ground hash or high-quality cannabis
- 6 ounces desiccated coconut
- 5 ounces small white marshmallow s

Directions:

a) After melting the butter in a pan, mix in your cocoa, milk, sugar and hash. Continue to heat, stirring on occasion, until contents are melted together. Be very careful that you do not boil it.
b) Remove from the heat and add the majority of the coconut, saving just enough for a final coating. Now divide your mixture into 15 similarly size balls, and then flatten them just enough to be wrapped around a marshmallow.
c) Once encasing a marshmallow, roll each of them in your remaining coconut until a generous coating has been applied.
d) We recommend only eating 1-2 per person, despite their tastiness.

40. Peanut Butter Goo Balls

Yield: 15 Goo Balls

Ingredients:

a) 250 g melted butter
b) 225 g oats
c) 250 g peanut butter
d) 3 tablespoon honey
e) 2 tablespoon ground cinnamo n
f) 2 tablespoon cocoa powder

Directions:

a) Place all ingredients in one large bowl and stir until everything is mixed in.
b) Place the mix into the freezer and leave it for 10-20 minutes.
c) Mold the mixture into individual balls, to the size of your preference. After which, drop it onto some waxpaper to set.
d) Some people prefer adding other ingredients such as chopped walnuts, raisins, Rice Krispies or Corn Flakes, just to experiment.
e) More oats can be added if you find the end result a little too sticky and gooey, or add more honey or peanut butter if it turns out to be too dry. It is all about being creative and adding your own touch to this delicacy.
f) Once that is done, you are now ready to serve this scrumptious treat, which can be eaten for dessert, a snack, or just any time of the day you choose to have an edible.
g) Enjoy!

41. Snowballs

Preparation Time: 1 ½ hr.
Cooking Time: 20-25 minutes
Servings: 12

Ingredients:

8. 1 cup butter, softened
9. 1/4 cup sugar
10. 1 tsp. pure vanilla extract
11. 2 cups all-purpose flour
12. 2 Tbsp. cornstarch
13. 1 cup of unsalted roasted almonds, finely chopped
14. 1/4 tsp. salt
15. 1 cup of powdered sugar to coat

Directions:

- By utilizing a stand mixer or a hand mixer, beat the butter with 1/4 cup of the sugar until creamy. Add the vanilla extract. Gently beat in the flour, corn starch, roasted almonds and salt until well combined. Wrap in plastic wrap and refrigerate for one hour. Preheat oven to 325°.Take the chilled dough out from the fridge and get about a tbsp. of dough then shape it into a 1-inch ball.
- Arrange the balls on the baking sheet about 1 inch apart. Bake the cookies on the middle shelf of the oven for 20 minutes, or until golden and set. Fill a shallow bowl with 1 cup of sifted powdered sugar. Cool for around 5 minutes, and when cool enough to touch, roll the cookies in the powdered sugar and set aside on the parchment-lined rack to cool completely. When cool, dust again in the powdered sugar and store in an airtight container.

DESSERT FAT BOMBS

- **Neapolitan fat bombs**

  INGREDIENTS
- 1/2 cup Butter
- 1/2 cup Coconut Oil
- 1/2 cup Sour Cream
- 1/2 cup Cream Cheese
- 2 tbsp. Erythritol
- 25 drops Liquid Stevia
- 2 tbsp. Cocoa Powder
- 1 tsp. Vanilla Extract
- 2 medium Strawberries

  DIRECTIONS
- In a bowl, combine butter, coconut oil, sour cream, cream cheese, erythritol, and liquid stevia.
- Using an immersion blender, blend together the ingredients into a smooth mixture.
- Divide the mixture into 3 different bowls. Add cocoa powder to one bowl, strawberries to another bowl, and vanilla to the last bowl.
- Mix together all of the ingredients again using an immersion blender. Separate the chocolate mixture into a container with a spout.
- Pour chocolate mixture into fat bomb mold. Place in freezer for 30 minutes, then repeat with the vanilla mixture.
- Freeze vanilla mixture for 30 minutes, then repeat process with strawberry mixture. Freeze again for at least 1 hour.
- Once they're completely frozen, remove from the fat bomb molds.

- **Maple & bacon fat pops**

INGREDIENTS

1. 2 tablespoon Coconut butter
2. Maple Bacon Cake Pops
3. 6 Oz. Burgers' Smokehouse Country Bacon
4. 5 large Eggs, separated
5. 1/4 cup Maple Syrup
6. 1/2 tsp. Vanilla Extract
7. 1/4 Cup Erythritol
8. 1/4 tsp. Liquid Stevia
9. 1 cup Honeyville Almond Flour
10. 2 tbsp. Psyllium Husk Powder
11. 1 tsp. Baking Powder
12. 1/2 tsp. Cream of Tartar
13. Salted Caramel Glaze 5 tbsp. Butter
14. 5 tbsp. Heavy Cream
15. 2 1/2 tbsp. Torani Sugar Free Salted Caramel

DIRECTIONS

1. Slice 6 Oz. Burgers' Smokehouse Country Bacon into small bite size chunks.
2. Either freezing the bacon for 30 minutes prior, or using scissors normally helps with this process.
3. Heat a pan to medium-high heat and cook the bacon until crisp.
4. Once crisp, remove the bacon from the pan and allow to dry on paper towels. Save excess bacon grease to sauté vegetables or other meats in it.
5. Preheat oven to 325F. In 2 separate bowls, separate the egg yolks from the egg whites of 5 large eggs.
6. In the bowl with the egg yolks, add 1/4 cup maple syrup,1/4 cup erythritol, 1/4 tsp. liquid stevia, and 1/2 tsp. vanilla extract.
7. Using a hand mixer, mix this together for about 2 minutes. The egg yolks should become lighter in color.

8. Add 1 cup Honeyville almond flour, 2 tbsp. Psyllium husk powder, 2 tbsp. coconut butter, and 1 tsp. baking powder.
9. Mix this again until a thick batter forms.
10. Wash off the whisks of the hand mixer in the sink to make sure all traces of fats are washed off of the whisks.
11. Add 1/2 tsp. cream of tartar to the egg whites.
12. Whisk the egg whites using a hand mixer until solid peaks form.
13. Add 2/3 crisped bacon into the cake pop batter.
14. Add about 1/3 of the egg whites into the batter and aggressively mix together.

a) Coconut orange fat bombs

INGREDIENTS

a) 1/2 cup Coconut Oil
b) 1/2 cup Heavy Whipping Cream
c) 4 oz. Cream Cheese
d) 1 tsp. Orange Vanilla Mio
e) drops Liquid Stevia

DIRECTIONS

1. Measure out coconut oil, heavy cream, and cream cheese.
2. Use an immersion blender to blend together all of the ingredients. If you're having a hard time blending the ingredients, you can microwave them for 30 seconds to 1 minute to soften them up.
3. Add Orange Vanilla Mio and liquid stevia into the mixture, and mix together with a spoon.
4. Spread the mixture into a silicone tray (Mine is an awesome Avenger's Ice Cube Tray) and freeze for 2-3 hours.
5. Once hardened, remove from the silicone tray and store in the freezer. Enjoy!

a) Jalapeno bombs

INGREDIENTS

- 1 cup butter, softened
- 3 oz. Cream Cheese
- 3 slices Bacon
- 1 medium Jalapeno Pepper
- 1/2 tsp. Dried Parsley
- 1/4 tsp. Onion Powder
- 1/4 tsp. Garlic Powder
- Salt and Pepper to Taste

DIRECTIONS

- Fry 3 slices of bacon in a pan until crisp.
- Remove bacon from the pan, but keep the remaining grease for later use.
- Wait until bacon is cooled and crisp.
- De-seed a jalapeno pepper, and then dice into small pieces.
- Combine cream cheese, butter, jalapeno, and spices. Season with salt and pepper to taste.
- Add the bacon fat in and mix together until a solid mixture is formed.
- Crumble bacon and set on a plate. Roll cream cheese mixture into balls using your hand, and then roll the ball into the bacon.

1. **Pizza fat bombs**

INGREDIENTS

- 4 oz. Cream Cheese
- slices Pepperoni
- pitted Black Olives
- 2 tbsp. Sun Dried Tomato Pesto

DIRECTIONS

a) Dice pepperoni and olives into small pieces.
b) Mix together basil, tomato pesto, and cream cheese.
c) Add the olives and pepperoni into the cream cheese and mix again.
d) Form into balls, then garnish with pepperoni, basil, and olive.

2. Peanut butter fat bombs

INGREDIENTS

- 1/2 CUP Coconut Oil
- 1/4 cup Cocoa Powder
- tbsp. PB Fit Powder
- tbsp. Shelled Hemp Seeds
- 2 tbsp. Heavy Cream
- 1 tsp. Vanilla Extract
- 28 drops Liquid Stevia
- 1/4 cup Unsweetened Shredded Coconut

DIRECTIONS

1. Mix together all of the dry ingredients with the coconut oil. It may take a bit of work, but it will eventually turn into a paste.
2. Add heavy cream, vanilla, and liquid stevia. Mix again until everything is combined and slightly creamy.
3. Measure out unsweetened shredded coconut on to a plate.

4. Roll balls out using your hand and then roll in the unsweetened shred-ded coconut. Lay on to a baking tray covered in parchment paper. Set in the freezer for about 20 minutes.

- **Maple pecan fat bomb bars**

  INGREDIENTS

a) 2 cups Pecan Halves
b) 1 cup Almond Flour
c) 1/2 cup Golden Flaxseed Meal
d) 1/2 cup Unsweetened Shredded Coconut
e) 1/2 cup Coconut Oil
f) 1/4 cup "Maple Syrup"
g) 1/4 tsp. Liquid Stevia (~25 drops)

DIRECTIONS

1. Measure out 2 cups of pecan halves and bake for 6-8 minutes at 350F in the oven. Just enough to when they start becoming aromatic.
2. Remove pecans from the oven, then add to a plastic bag. Use a rolling pin to crush them into chunks. It doesn't matter too much about the consistency,
3. Mix the dry ingredients into a bowl: 1 cup Almond Flour, 1/2 cup Golden Flaxseed Meal, and 1/2 cup Unsweetened Shredded Coconut.
4. Add the crushed pecans to the bowl and mix together again.
5. Finally, add the 1/2 cup Coconut Oil, 1/4 cup "Maple Syrup" (recipe here), and 1/4 tsp. Liquid Stevia. Mix this together well until a crumbly dough is for-med.
6. Press the dough into a casserole dish. I am using an 11×7 baking dish for this.
7. Bake for 20-25 minutes at 350F, or until the edges are lightly browned.
8. Remove from the oven; allow partially cooling, and refrigerating for at least 1 hour (to cut cleanly).
9. Cut into 12 slices and remove using a spatula.

- **Cheesy bacon bombs**

INGREDIENTS

- 3 oz. Mozzarella Cheese
- tbsp. Almond Flour
- tbsp. Butter, melted
- 3 tbsp. Psyllium Husk Powder
- 1 large Egg
- 1/4 tsp. Salt
- 1/4 tsp. Fresh Ground Black pepper
- 1/8 tsp. Garlic Powder
- 1/8 tsp. Onion Powder
- slices Bacon
- 1 cup Oil, Lard or Tallow (for frying)

DIRECTIONS

1. Add 4 oz. (half) Mozzarella cheese to a bowl.
2. Microwave 4 tbsp. butter for 15-20 seconds or until it is melted completely.
3. Microwave cheese for 45-60 seconds until melted and gooey (should be a
4. Add 1 egg and butter to the mixture and mix well.
5. Add 4 tbsp. almond flour, 3 tbsp. Psyllium husk, and the rest of your spices to the mixture (1/4 tsp. Salt, 1/4 tsp. Fresh Ground Black pepper, 1/8 tsp. Garlic Powder, and 1/8 tsp. Onion Powder).
6. Mix everything together and dump it out onto a silpat. Roll the dough out, or using your hands, form dough into a rectangle.
7. Spread the rest of the cheese over half of the dough and fold the dough over lengthwise.
8. Fold the dough again vertically so you form a square shape.

9. Crimp the edges using your fingers and press the dough together into a rectangle. You want the filling to be tight inside.
10. Using a knife, cut the dough into 20 squares.
11. Cut each slice of bacon in half, and then lay the square at the end of 1 piece of bacon.
12. Roll the dough into the bacon tightly until the ends are overlapping. You can "stretch" your bacon if you need to before rolling.
13. Use a toothpick to secure the bacon after you roll it.
14. Do this for every piece of dough that you have. At the end you will have 20 cheesy bacon bombs.
15. Heat up oil, lard, or tallow to 350-375F and then fry the cheesy bacon bombs 3 or 4 pieces at a time.

- **Caramel bacon Fat Pop**

  INGREDIENTS
- Maple Bacon Cake Pops
- 6 Oz. Burgers' Smokehouse Country Bacon
- 5 large Eggs, seperated 1/4 cup Maple Syrup (recipe here)
- 1/2 tsp. Vanilla Extract 1/4 Cup NOW Erythritol 1/4 tsp. Liquid Stevia
- 1 cup Honeyville Almond Flour
- 2 tbsp. Psyllium Husk Powder
- 1 tsp. Baking Powder
- 2 tbsp. Butter
- 1/2 tsp. Cream of Tartar
- Salted Caramel Glaze 5 tbsp. Butter
- 5 tbsp. Heavy Cream
- 2 1/2 tbsp. Torani Sugar Free Salted Caramel

DIRECTIONS

a) Slice 6 Oz. Burgers' Smokehouse Country Bacon into small bite size chunks.
b) Either freezing the bacon for 30 minutes prior, or using scissors normally helps with this process.
c) Heat a pan to medium-high heat and cook the bacon until crisp.
d) Once crisp, remove the bacon from the pan and allow to dry on paper towels. Save excess bacon grease to sauté vegetables or other meats in it.
e) Preheat oven to 325F. In 2 separate bowls, separate the egg yolks from the egg whites of 5 large eggs.
f) In the bowl with the egg yolks, add 1/4 cup maple syrup (recipe here), 1/4 cup erythritol, 1/4 tsp. liquid stevia, and 1/2 tsp. vanilla extract.
g) Using a hand mixer, mix this together for about 2 minutes. The egg yolks should become lighter in color.

h) Add 1 cup Honeyville almond flour, 2 tbsp. Psyllium husk powder, 2 tbsp. butter, and 1 tsp. baking powder.
i) Mix this again until a thick batter forms.
j) Wash off the whisks of the hand mixer in the sink to make sure all traces of fats are washed off of the whisks.
k) Add 1/2 tsp. cream of tartar to the egg whites.
l) Whisk the egg whites using a hand mixer until solid peaks form.
m) Add 2/3 crisped bacon into the cake pop batter.
n) Add about 1/3 of the egg whites into the batter and aggressively mix together.
o)

3. Salted caramel cashew bars

Ingredients:

- 2 cups all-purpose flour
- ½ tsp. baking powder
- ½ tsp. salt
- 12 TBSP. butter, at room temperature
- 6 TBSP. unsalted butter, cut into chunks
- 1 cup light brown sugar, firmly packed
- 1 large egg
- 3 tsp. vanilla extract
- 1½ cups granulated sugar
- 1 cup heavy cream
- 2 cups salted, roasted cashews

p) Heat the oven to 340°F (171°C). Line a 9×13-inch (23×33cm) baking pan with parchment paper and set aside. In a small bowl, combine all-purpose flour, baking powder, and ¼ teaspoon salt. Set aside.

q) In a medium bowl, mix 6 tablespoons butter, unsalted butter, and light brown sugar with an electric mixer at medium speed for 5 minutes until light and fluffy. Add egg and 1 teaspoon vanilla extract, and beat for 2 minutes at low speed until combined.

r) Add flour mixture and beat at medium speed for 2 to 3 minutes. Press crust mixture into the prepared pan. Chill for 30 minutes.

s) In a medium nonstick pan over medium heat, heat granulated sugar. When you see sugar beginning to color, stir until it's light brown, about 5 to 7 minutes. Carefully add heavy cream and stir until smooth.

t) Turn down the heat to low and add remaining 6 tablespoons butter, remaining 2 teaspoons vanilla extract, and remaining ¼ teaspoon salt. Stir until butter has melted and remove from the heat.

u) Stir cashews into caramel mixture. Pour caramel-cashew mixture into the pan on top of chilled crust. Bake for 20 minutes until set. Allow to cool thoroughly before cutting.

4. Pistachio caramels

Ingredients:

- ½ cup butter
- 2 cups dark brown sugar, firmly packed
- ½ cup dark corn syrup
- 2 cups heavy cream
- ¼ tsp. salt
- 1 cup chopped pistachios, roasted
- 2 tsp. vanilla extract

Directions

h) Line an 8-inch (20cm) square pan with aluminum foil, spray with nonstick cooking spray, and set aside.

i) In a medium saucepan over low heat, melt butter. Add dark brown sugar, dark corn syrup, 1 cup heavy cream, and salt. Bring to a boil, stirring occasionally, for 12 to 15 minutes or until mixture reaches 225°F (110°C) on a candy thermometer.

j) Slowly add remaining 1 cup heavy cream. Bring mixture to a boil and cook for 15 more minutes or until it reaches 250°F (120°C). Remove from heat and add pistachios and vanilla extract. Pour into the prepared pan.

k) Cool for at least 3 hours before removing from the foil and cutting into 48 pieces.

l) Cut wax paper into 48 3-inch (7.5cm) squares. Place each caramel in the center of a wax paper square, roll up the paper around caramel, and twist the ends of the paper.

5. Key lime squares

Ingredients:

- 4 TBSP. unsalted butter, at room temperature
- 4 TBSP. butter, at room temperature
- ½ cup confectioners' sugar
- 2 cups plus 5 TBSP. all-purpose flour
- 1 tsp. vanilla extract
- Pinch salt
- 4 large eggs, lightly beaten
- 1¾ cups granulated sugar
- ¼ cup Key lime juice
- 1 TBSP. grated lime zest

Directions

15. Heat the oven to 340°F (171°C). Lightly coat a 9×13-inch (23×33cm) baking pan with nonstick cooking spray and set aside.
16. In a large bowl, beat unsalted butter, butter, and confectioners' sugar with an electric mixer at medium speed for 3 to 4 minutes or until light and fluffy.
17. Add all-purpose flour, vanilla extract, and salt, and mix for 2 to 3 more minutes or until well combined.
18. Press dough into the bottom of the prepared pan. Bake for 20 to 23 minutes, until light golden brown. Allow crust to cool for 10 minutes.
19. In a large bowl, whisk together eggs and granulated sugar. Add Key lime juice and lime zest, and whisk well.
20. Pour mixture over cooled crust and bake for 23 to 25 minutes or until set. Cool fully before cutting into 12 squares.
21. Storage: Keep tightly wrapped in plastic wrap in the refrigerator for up to 5 days.

6. White chocolate granola bites

Ingredients:

- 1½ cups granola
- 3 TBSP. butter, melted
- 2 cups white chocolate melts

Directions

6. Heat the oven to 250°F (120°C). On a rimmed baking sheet, mix granola and 2 tablespoons butter. Place the baking sheet in the oven for 5 minutes.
7. Remove the baking sheet and stir until granola is completely mixed with butter. Return the baking sheet to the oven for 15 minutes, stirring every 5 minutes. Remove from the oven and allow granola to cool completely.
8. In a double boiler over medium heat, combine white chocolate melts and remaining 1 tablespoon butter. Stir for 5 to 7 minutes, or until white chocolate is fully melted and thoroughly combined with butter. Remove from heat.
9. Stir cooled granola into white chocolate mixture. Drop by heaping tablespoons onto parchment paper and allow to cool fully before serving.
10. Storage: Keep in an airtight container at room temperature for up to 1 week.

7. Candied bacon toffee squares

Ingredients:

- 8 slices bacon
- ¼ cup light brown sugar, firmly packed
- 8 TBSP. butter, softened
- 2 TBSP. unsalted butter, softened
- ⅓ cup dark brown sugar, firmly packed
- ⅓ cup confectioners' sugar
- 1½ cups all-purpose flour
- ½ tsp. salt
- ½ cup toffee bits
- 1 cup dark chocolate chips
- ⅓ cup chopped almonds

Directions

6. Heat the oven to 350°F (180°C). In a medium bowl, toss bacon and light brown sugar, and arrange in a single layer on a baking sheet.
7. Bake for 20 to 25 minutes or until bacon is golden and crispy. Remove from the oven and allow to cool for 15 to 20 minutes. Chop into small pieces.
8. Reduce the oven temperature to 340°F (171°C). Line a 9×13-inch (23×33cm) baking pan with aluminum foil, spray with nonstick cooking spray, and set aside.
9. In a large bowl, mix butter, unsalted butter, dark brown sugar, and confectioners' sugar with an electric mixer at medium speed until light and fluffy. Add all-purpose flour and salt gradually, mixing until just combined. Stir in ¼ cup toffee bits until they're distributed evenly.
10. Press dough into the prepared pan and bake for 25 minutes or until golden brown. Remove from the oven, sprinkle with dark chocolate chips, and leave for 3 minutes or until chips are softened.
11. Spread softened chocolate evenly on top and sprinkle with almonds, candied bacon, and remaining ¼ cup toffee bits.

Allow to cool for 2 hours or until chocolate is set. Cut into 16 2-inch (5cm) squares.

12. Storage: Keep in an airtight container in the refrigerator for up to 1 week.

8. Caramel Walnut Dream Bars

Ingredients:

- 1 box yellow cake mix
- 3 tablespoons butter softened
- 1 egg
- 14 ounces sweetened condensed milk
- 1 egg
- 1 teaspoon pure vanilla extract
- 1/2 cup walnuts finely ground
- 1/2 cup finely ground toffee bits

Directions:

h) Preheat oven to 350. Prepare rectangular cake pan with cooking spray then set aside.

i) Combine cake mix, butter and one egg in a mixing bowl then mix until crumbly. Press mixture onto bottom of prepared pan then set aside.

j) In another mixing bowl combine milk, remaining egg, extract, walnuts and toffee bits.

k) Mix well and pour over base in pan. Bake for 35 minutes.

9. Chronic pecan bars

INGREDIENTS

- 2 cups Pecan Halves
- 1 cup Cassava Flour
- 1/2 cup Golden Flaxseed Meal
- 1/2 cup Unsweetened Shredded Coconut
- 1/2 cup Cana-Coconut Oil
- 1/4 cup Honey
- 1/4 tsp. Liquid Stevia

DIRECTIONS

16. Measure out 2 cups of pecan halves and bake for 6-8 minutes at 350F in the oven. Just enough to when they start becoming aromatic.
17. Remove pecans from the oven, and then add to a plastic bag. Use a rolling pin to crush them into chunks. It doesn't matter too much about the consistency,
18. Mix the dry ingredients into a bowl: 1 cup Cassava Flour, 1/2 cup Golden Flaxseed Meal, and 1/2 cup Unsweetened Shredded Coconut.
19. Add the crushed pecans to the bowl and mix together again.
20. Finally, add the 1/2 cup Cana Coconut Oil, 1/4 cup honey and 1/4 tsp. Liquid Stevia. Mix this together well until a crumbly dough is formed.
21. Press the dough into a casserole dish.
22. Bake for 20-25 minutes at 350F, or until the edges are lightly browned.
23. Remove from the oven; allow partially cooling, and refrigerating for at least 1 hour.
24. Cut into 12 slices and remove using a spatula.

16. Almond butter chia squares

INGREDIENTS

- 1/2 cup Raw Almonds
- 1 tbsp. + 1 tsp. Coconut Oil
- tbsp. NOW Erythritol
- 2 tbsp. Butter
- 1/4 cup Heavy Cream
- 1/4 tsp. Liquid Stevia
- 1 1/2 tsp. Vanilla Extract

DIRECTIONS

4 Add 1/2 cup Raw Almonds to a pan and toast for about 7 minutes on medium-low heat. Just enough so that you start to smell the nuttiness coming out.

5 Add the nuts to the food processor and grind them.

6 Once they reach a mealy consistency, add 2 tbsp. NOW Erythritol and 1 tsp. Coconut Oil.

7 Continue grinding almonds until almond butter is formed butter is browned.

8 Once butter is browned, add 1/4 cup Heavy Cream, 2 tbsp. NOW Erythritol, 1/4 tsp. Liquid Stevia, and 1 1/2 tsp. Vanilla Extract to the butter. Turn heat to low and stir well as the cream bubbles.

9 Grind 1/4 Cup Chia Seeds in a spice grinder until a powder is formed.

10 Begin toasting chia seeds and 1/2 Cup Unsweetened Shredded Coconut Flakes in a pan on medium low. You want the coconut to just slightly brown.

11 Add almond butter to the butter and heavy cream mixture and stir it in well. Let it cook down into a paste.

12 In a square (or whatever size you want) baking dish, add the almond butter mixture, toasted chia and coconut mixture, and 1/2 Cup Coconut Cream. You can add the coconut cream to a pan to melt it slightly before adding it.
13 Add 1 tbsp. Coconut oil and 2 tbsp. Coconut Flour and mix everything together well.
14 Using your fingers, pack the mixture into the baking dish well.
15 Refrigerate mixture for at least an hour and then take it out of the baking dish. It should hold form now.
16 Chop the mixture into squares or any shape you'd like and put back in the refrigerator for at least a few more hours. You can use excess mixture to form more squares, but I ate it instead.
17 Take out and snack on it as you want!

16. **Chia seed Nuggets**

INGREDIENTS

- 2 Tablespoons coconut oil
- 1/2 cup Chia Seeds, ground
- 3 oz. Shredded Cheddar Cheese
- 1 1/4 cup Ice Water
- 2 tbsp. Psyllium Husk Powder
- 1/4 tsp. Xanthan Gum
- 1/4 tsp. Garlic Powder
- 1/4 tsp. Onion Powder
- 1/4 tsp. Oregano
- 1/4 tsp. Paprika
- 1/4 tsp. Salt
- 1/4 tsp. Pepper

DIRECTIONS

5. Preheat oven to 375F. Grind 1/2 cup Chia Seeds in a spice grinder. You want a meal like texture.
6. Add ground Chia Seeds, 2 tbsp. Psyllium Husk Powder, 1/4 tsp. Xanthan Gum, 1/4 tsp. Garlic Powder, 1/4 tsp. Onion Powder, 1/4 tsp. Oregano, 1/4 tsp. Paprika, 1/4 tsp. Salt and 1/4 tsp. Pepper to a bowl. Mix this together well.
7. Add 2 tbsp. Coconut oil to the dry ingredients and mix it together. It should turn into the consistency of wet sand.
8. Add 1 1/4 cup ice cold water to the bowl. Mix it together very well. You may need to spend extra time mixing it together as the chia seeds and Psyllium take a little bit of time to absorb the water. Keep mixing until solid dough is formed.
9. Grate 3 oz. Cheddar Cheese and add it to the bowl.
10. Using your hands, knead the dough together. You want it to be relatively dry and not sticky by the time you finish.
11. Put the dough onto a silpat and let it sit for a few minutes.

12. Spread or roll the dough out thin so that it covers the entire silpat. If you can get it thinner, keep rolling and save the excess for a second cook.
13. Bake for 30-35 minutes in the oven until cooked.
14. Taken them out of the oven, and while hot, cut into individual crackers.
15. You can either use the blunt edge of a knife (don't cut into the silicone), or a large spatula.
16. Put the crackers back into the oven for 5-7 minutes on broil or until the tops are browned and well crisped. Remove from the oven and set on a rack to cool. As they cool, they get crisper.
17. Serve up with your favorite sauces. I'm using my Roasted Garlic Chipotle Aioli.

18. Chocolate Protein Nut Bars

Servings: 12 bars Preparation time: 1 hour

Ingredients:

- 100% pure nut butter, 250 g
- Roasted wattles seed, 1 ½ teaspoon
- Fat-free plain yoghurt, 110 g
- 100% Whey protein powder, 100 g
- Cinnamon, 1 ½ teaspoons
- Raw cacao nibs, 4 teaspoons
- 85% dark chocolate, 100 g
- Pure vanilla extract, 1 tablespoon
- 100% Pea protein powder, 30 g

Method:

e) Add all the ingredients except chocolate to food processor and pulse until smooth.

f) Make 12 bars from the mixture and refrigerate them for 30 minutes.

g) When the bars are firm, melt chocolate in microwave and dip each bar into it and coat well.

h) Arrange coated bars on a lined sheet and refrigerate again for 30 minutes or until the chocolate is firm.

i) Enjoy.

19. German Chocolate Protein Bars

Servings: 12 bars

Preparation time: 2 hours 20 minutes

Ingredients:

- Oats, 1 cup
- Shredded coconut, ½ cup + ¼ cup, divided
- Soy protein powder, ½ cup
- Pecans, ½ cup + ¼ cup, chopped, divided
- Water, up to ¼ cup
- Cocoa powder, ¼ cup
- Vanilla extract, 1 teaspoon
- Cacao nibs, 2 tablespoons
- Salt, ¼ teaspoon
- Medjool dates, 1 cup, pitted and soaked for 30 minutes

Method:

i) Process oats until fine flour then add cocoa powder and protein powder, process again.

j) Meanwhile drain the dates and add them to the food processor. Pulse for 30 seconds then add ½ cup shredded coconut and ½ cup pecan followed by salt and vanilla.

k) Process again and keep adding water little by little and form dough.

l) Place dough in a large bowl and add remaining pecans and coconut followed by cacao nibs.

m) Place dough on parchment paper and cover it with another parchment and form a thick square.

n) Refrigerate for 2 hours then remove parchment paper and slice into 12 bars of your desired length.

20. Blueberry Bliss Protein Bars

Ingredients:

- 100% pure uncontaminated rolled oats, 1 + ½ cups
- Pepitas, 1/3 cup
- Whole almonds, ¾ cup
- Unsweetened apple sauce ¼ cup
- Dried blueberries, ½ heaping cup
- Sunflower seeds, ¼ cup
- Almond butter, 1 cup
- Maple syrup, 1/3 cup
- Walnuts, 1/3 cup
- Pistachios, ½ cup
- Ground flaxseed, 1/3 cup

Method:

p) Line a baking pan with wax paper and keep aside.

q) In a large bowl combine roll oats, almonds, sunflower seeds, dried berries, walnuts, pistachios, flaxseeds and pepitas.

r) Drizzle apple sauce and maple syrup on top and mix well.

s) Now add butter and combine well.

t) Transfer batter to the pan and even it out from top.

u) Freeze for an hour. When the mixture is completely set flip it out on counter.

v) Slice in your desired thickens and length into 16 bars.

21. Chocolate Chip Peanut ButterProtein Bars

Ingredients:

- Coconut flour, ¼ cup
- Vanilla crème stevia, 1 teaspoon
- Peanut flour, 6 tablespoons
- Vanilla extract, 1 teaspoon
- Salt, ¼ teaspoon
- Miniature chocolate chips, 1 tablespoon
- Coconut oil, 1 teaspoon, melted and cooled slightly
- Soy protein isolate, 6 tablespoons
- Unsweetened cashew milk, ½ cup + 2 tablespoons

Method:

h) Line a loaf pan with wax paper. Keep aside.
i) Combine both flours with soy protein and salt.
j) In another bowl stir coconut milk with stevia, cashew milk and vanilla. Pour this mixture gradually in the flour mixture and whisk well to combine.
k) Now add ½ chocolate chips and gently fold them in the mixture.
l) Transfer the mixture to prepared loaf pan and spread evenly using a spatula.
m) Top with remaining chocolate chips and freeze for 3 hours.
n) Slice into desired thickness and length.

PURE
VANILLA

22. Raw Pumpkin Hemp SeedProtein Bars

Ingredients:

- Medjool dates, ½ cup, pitted
- Vanilla extract, ½ teaspoon
- Pumpkin seeds, ¼ cup
- Salt, ¼ teaspoon
- Cinnamon, ½ teaspoon
- Hemp seed butter, ½ cup
- Nutmeg, ¼ teaspoon
- Water, ¼ cup
- Raw oats, 2 cups
- Chia seeds, 2 tablespoons

Method:

g) Line a baking pan with parchment paper and keep aside, Soak dates for 30 minutes then blend until smooth.

h) Transfer the mixture to a bowl and add hemp butter and combine well.

i) Now add remaining ingredients and gently fold in to incorporate well.

j) Transfer to the pan and even out using a spatula.

k) Place in the fridge for 2 hours then slice into 16 bars.

23. Ginger Vanilla Protein CrunchBars

Ingredients:

- Butter, 2 tablespoons
- Oats, 1 cup
- Raw almonds, ½ cup, chopped
- Coconut milk, ¼ cup
- Shredded coconut, ¼ cup
- Protein powder (Vanilla), 2 scoops
- Maple syrup, ¼ cup
- Crystalized ginger, ½ cup, chopped
- Corn flakes, 1 cup, pounded to bulky crumbs Sunflower seeds, ¼ cup

Method:

b) Melt butter in a pan and add maple syrup. Stir well.

c) Add milk followed by protein powder and stir well to combine. When the mixture changes to a smooth consistency turn off the heat.

d) In a large bowl add sunflower seeds, almonds, oats, cornflakes and ¾ ginger pieces.

e) Pour the mixture on the dry ingredients and combine well.

f) Transfer to a wax paper prepared loaf pan and spread in an even layer.

g) Top with remaining ginger and coconut.Bake for 20 minutes at 325 F. Let it cool before slicing.

24. Peanut Butter Pretzel Bars

Ingredients:

- Soy crisps, 5 cups
- Water, ½ cup
- Mini pretzel twists, 6, roughly chopped
- Powdered peanut butter, 6 tablespoons
- Peanuts, 2 tablespoons, roughly chopped
- Soy protein powder, 6 tablespoons
- Peanut butter chips, 2 tablespoons, cut in half Agave, 6 tablespoons

Method:

g) Spray a baking pan with cooking spray and keep aside.
h) Process soy crisps in food processor and add to a bowl.
i) Add protein powder and mix.
j) Heat a saucepan and add water, agave and powdered butter. Stir while cooking on medium heat for 5 minutes. Let the mixture boil for a few seconds then and soy mixture while stirring constantly.
k) Transfer the mixture to prepared pan and top with pretzels, peanuts and peanut butter chips.
l) Refrigerate until firm. Cut into bars and enjoy.

Melissa's Southern Style Kitchen

25. Cranberry Almond ProteinBars

.Ingredients:

- Roasted sea salt almonds, 2 cups
- Unsweetened coconut flakes, ½ cup
- Puffed rice cereal, 2/3 cups
- Vanilla extract, 1 teaspoon
- Dried cranberries, 2/3 cups
- Hemp seeds, 1 heaping tablespoon
- Brown rice syrup, 1/3 cup Honey, 2 tablespoons

Method:

b) Combine almonds with cranberries, hemp seeds, rice cereal and coconut. Keep aside.

c) In a saucepan add honey followed by vanilla and rice syrup. Stir and boil for 5 minutes.

d) Pour the sauce over dry ingredients and stir quickly to combine.

e) Transfer the mixture to a prepared baking sheet and spread in an even layer.

f) Refrigerate for 30 minutes.

g) When they are set, slice them into bars of your desired size and enjoy.

26. Triple Chocolate Protein CakeBars

Ingredients:

- Oat flour, 1 cup
- Baking soda, ½ teaspoon
- Almond milk, ¼ cup
- Chocolate whey protein powder, 1 scoop
- Stevia baking blend, ¼ cup
- Almond flour, ¼ cup
- Dark chocolate chips, 3 tablespoons
- Salt, ¼ teaspoon
- Walnuts, 3 tablespoons, chopped
- Unsweetened dark cocoa powder, 3 tablespoons
- Unsweetened apple sauce, 1/3 cup
- Egg, 1
- Plain Greek yogurt, ¼ cup
- Liquid egg whites, 2 tablespoons
- Vanilla whey protein powder, 1 scoop

Method:

f) Preheat oven to 350 F.

g) Grease a baking pan with cooking spray and keep aside.

h) In a large bowl combine both flours with salt, baking soda, both protein powders and dark cocoa powder. Keep aside.

i) In another bowl whisk eggs with stevia and whisk until well combined then add remaining wet ingredients and whisk again.

j) Gradually stir wet mixture into dry mixture and whisk well to combine.

k) Add walnuts and chocolate chips, gently fold them it.

l) Transfer the mixture to prepared pan and bake for 25 minutes.

m) Let cool before removing from the pan and slicing

27. Raspberry-Chocolate Bars

Ingredients:

- Peanut or almond butter, ½ cup
- Flaxseed, ¼ cup
- Blue agave, 1/3 cup
- Chocolate protein powder, ¼ cup
- Raspberries, ½ cup
- Instant rolled oats, 1 cup

Method:

d) Combine peanut butter with agave and cook over low heat, stirring constantly.
e) When the mixture form a smooth texture add it to the oats, flaxseed and protein. Mix well.
f) Add raspberries and gently fold it.
g) Transfer the batter to prepared pan and freeze for an hour.
h) Slice into 8 bars when firm and enjoy.

28. Peanut Butter Cookie Dough Bars

Ingredients:

- Rolled oats, ¼ cup
- Peanut butter, 3 tablespoons
- Protein powder, ½ cup
- Salt, a pinch
- Large Medjool dates, 10
- Raw cashews, 1 cup
- Maple syrup, 2 tablespoons Whole peanuts, for garnish

Method:

u) Pulse oats in food processor into fine flour.

v) Now add all the ingredients except whole peanuts and process until smooth.

w) Taste and make any adjustments if you like.

x) Transfer the mixture to a loaf pan and top with whole peanuts.

y) Refrigerate for 3 hours. When the mixture is firm, place it on kitchen counter and slice into 8 bars of your desired length.

29. Muesli Protein Bars

Ingredients:

- Unsweetened almond milk, ½ cup
- Honey, 3 tablespoons
- Quinoa, ¼ cup, cooked
- Chia seeds, 1 teaspoon
- Flour, 1 tablespoon
- Chocolate protein powder, 2 scoops
- Chocolate chips, ¼ cup
- Cinnamon, ½ teaspoon
- Ripe banana, ½, mashed
- Almonds, ¼ cup, sliced
- Muesli, 1 ½ cup, of your favorite brand

Method:

j) Preheat oven to 350 F.

k) Stir almond milk with banana mash, chia seeds and honey in a medium bowl and keep aside.

l) In another bowl combine remaining ingredients and toss well.

m) Now pour almond milk mixture over the dry ingredients and fold everything well.

n) Transfer the batter to a pan and bake for 20-25 minutes.

o) Let cool before removing from pan and slicing.

30. Carrot Cake Protein Bars

Ingredients:

For the Bars:

- Oat flour, 2 cups
- Dairy-free milk, 1 tablespoon
- Mixed spice, 1 teaspoon
- Vanilla protein powder, ½ cup
- Carrots, ½ cup, mashed
- Cinnamon, 1 tablespoon
- Coconut flour, ½ cup, sifted
- Brown rice syrup, ½ cup
- Granulated sweetener of choice, 2 tablespoons
- Almond butter, ¼ cup

For the Frosting:

- Vanilla protein powder, 1 scoop
- Coconut milk, 2-3 tablespoons
- Cream cheese, ¼ cup

Method:

f) To prepare protein bars combine flour with mixed spice, protein powder, cinnamon and sweetener.

g) In another but mix butter with liquid sweetener and microwave for a few seconds until melted.

h) Transfer this mixture to the flour bowl and mix well.

i) Now add carrots and fold gently.

j) Now gradually add milk, stirring constantly until required consistency is achieved.

k) Transfer to a prepared pan and refrigerate for 30 minutes.

l) Meanwhile prepare frosting and combine protein powder with cream cheese.

m) Gradually add milk and stir well to get desired texture.

n) When the mixture is set, slice into bars of your desired length and lather frosting over each bar.

31. Orange and Goji Berry Bars

Ingredients:

- Vanilla whey protein powder, ½ cup
- Orange rind, 1 tablespoon, grated
- Ground almonds, ¾ cup
- 85% dark chocolate, 40 g, melted
- Coconut milk, ¼ cup
- Coconut flour, ¼ cup
- Chili powder, 1 teaspoon
- Vanilla essence, 1 tablespoon
- Goji berries, ¾ cup

Method:

g) Combine protein powder with coconut flour in a bowl.
h) Add remaining ingredients to the flour mixture.
i) Stir milk and combine well.
j) Form bar shapes from the batter and arrange on a sheet.
k) Melt chocolate and cool it for a few minutes then dip each bar into melted chocolate and arrange on the baking sheet.
l) Refrigerate until the chocolate is completely firm.
m) Enjoy.

32. Strawberry Ripe Protein Bar

Ingredients:

- Freeze-Dried strawberries, 60 g
- Vanilla, ½ teaspoon
- Unsweetened shredded coconut, 60 g
- Unsweetened almond milk, 60 ml
- Unflavored Whey protein powder, 60 g Dark chocolate, 80 g

Method:

j) Process dried strawberries until grounded then add whey, vanilla and coconut. Process again until a fine grounded mixture is formed.

k) Stir milk in the mixture and process until everything is well incorporated.

l) Line a loaf pan with wax paper and transfer the mixture into it.

m) Use a spatula to evenly spread the mixture.

n) Refrigerate until the mixture is set.

o) Microwave dark chocolate for 30 seconds. Stir well until it's smooth and completely melted.

p) Let the chocolate cool slightly and in meantime slice the strawberry mixture into eight bars of your desired thickness.

q) Now one by one dip each bar into the chocolate and coat well.

r) Arrange coated bars on a line baking sheet. Once all the bars are coated, refrigerate them until the chocolate is set and firm.

33. Mocha Protein Bars

Ingredients:

- Almond flour, 30 g
- Coconut flour, 30 g
- Espresso, 60 g, freshly brewed and cooled
- Unflavored whey protein isolate, 60 g
- Coconut sugar, 20 g
- Unsweetened cocoa powder, 14 g
- Dark chocolate with 70%-85% cocoa solids, 48 g

Method:

d) Combine all the dry ingredients together.

e) Stir expresso and whisk well to combine leaving no lumps.

f) The mixture will turn into a smooth ball at this point.

g) Divide it into six pieces of equal size and form each piece into bar. Arrange the bars on a sheet and cover it with plastic. Refrigerate for an hour.

h) Once the bars are set, microwave dark chocolate and stir until melted.

i) Coat each bar into melted chocolate and arrange on wax lined baking sheet.

j) Drizzle remaining chocolate on top in a swirl pattern and refrigerate again until the chocolate is firm.

34. Banana Chocolate Protein Bars

Ingredients:

- Freeze-dried banana, 40g
- Almond milk, 30 ml
- Banana flavored protein powder isolate, 70 g
- 100% peanut butter, 25 g
- Gluten-free rolled oats, 30 g
- 100% chocolate, 40 g
- Sweetener, to taste

Method:

f) Ground banana in food processor. Now add protein powder and oats, process again until finely grounded.

g) Stir remaining ingredients except chocolate and process again until smooth.

h) Transfer the mixture to a lined loaf pan and cover with plastic. Refrigerate until firm.

i) When the bars are set, cut into four bars.

j) Now melt chocolate in microwave and let it cool slightly before dipping each banana bar into it. Coat well and refrigerate the bars again until the chocolate is firm.

35. Heavenly Raw Bars

Ingredients:

- Coconut milk, 2 tablespoons
- Unsweetened cocoa powder, as required
- Protein powder, 1 ½ scoops
- Flaxseed meal, 1 tablespoon

Method:

a) Combine all the ingredients together.
b) Grease a baking pan with far-free cooking spray and transfer the batter into it.
c) Let the mixture sit at room temperature until its firm.

36. Monster Bars

- 1/2 c. butter, softened
- 1 c. brown sugar, packed
- 1 c. sugar
- 1-1/2 c. creamy peanut butter
- 3 eggs, beaten
- 2 t. vanilla extract
- 2 t. baking soda
- 4-1/2 c. quick-cooking oats, uncooked
- 1 c. semi-sweet chocolate chips
- 1 c. candy-coated chocolates

g) In a large bowl, mix together all ingredients in order listed. Spread dough in a greased 15"x10" jelly-roll pan.
h) Bake at 350 degrees for 15 minutes, or until lightly golden.
i) Cool and cut into bars. Makes about 1-1/2 dozen.

37. Blueberry Crumble Bars

- 1-1/2 c. sugar, divided
- 3 c. all-purpose flour
- 1 t. baking powder
- 1/4 t. salt
- 1/8 t. cinnamon
- 1 c. shortening
- 1 egg, beaten
- 1 T. cornstarch
- 4 c. blueberries

a) Stir together one cup sugar, flour, baking powder, salt and cinnamon.

b) Use a pastry cutter or fork to cut in shortening and egg; dough will be crumbly.

c) Pat half of dough into a greased 13"x9" baking pan; set aside.

d) In a separate bowl, stir together cornstarch and remaining sugar; gently fold in berries.

e) Sprinkle blueberry mixture evenly over dough in pan.

f) Crumble remaining dough over top. Bake at 375 degrees for 45 minutes, or until top is lightly golden. Cool completely before cutting into squares. Makes one dozen.

38. Gumdrop Bars

- 1/2 c. butter, melted
- 1/2 t. baking powder
- 1-1/2 c. brown sugar, packed
- 1/2 t. salt
- 2 eggs, beaten
- 1/2 c. chopped nuts
- 1-1/2 c. all-purpose flour
- 1 c. gumdrops, chopped
- 1 t. vanilla extract
- Garnish: powdered sugar

f) In a large bowl, mix together all ingredients except powdered sugar.

g) Spread dough in a greased and floured 13"x9" baking pan. Bake at 350 degrees for 25 to 30 minutes, until golden.

h) Sprinkle with powdered sugar. Cool; cut into bars. Makes 2 dozen.

39. Salted Nut Roll Bars

- 18-1/2 oz. pkg. yellow cake mix
- 3/4 c. butter, melted and divided
- 1 egg, beaten
- 3 c. mini marshmallows
- 10-oz. pkg. peanut butter chips
- 1/2 c. light corn syrup
- 1 t. vanilla extract
- 2 c. salted peanuts
- 2 c. crispy rice cereal

b) In a bowl, mix together dry cake mix, 1/4 cup butter and egg; press dough into a greased 13"x9" baking pan. Bake at 350 degrees for 10 to 12 minutes.

c) Sprinkle marshmallows over baked crust; return to oven and bake for 3 additional minutes, or until marshmallows are melted. In a saucepan over medium heat, melt peanut butter chips, corn syrup, remaining butter and vanilla.

d) Stir in nuts and cereal. Spread peanut butter mixture over marshmallow layer. Chill until firm; cut into squares. Makes 2-1/2 dozen.

40. Black Forest Cherry Bars

- 3 21-oz. cans cherry pie filling, divided
- 18-1/2 oz. pkg. chocolate cake mix
- 1/4 c. oil
- 3 eggs, beaten
- 1/4 c. cherry-flavored brandy or cherry juice
- 6-oz. pkg. semi-sweet chocolate chips
- Optional: whipped topping

f) Refrigerate 2 cans of pie filling until chilled. Using an electric mixer on low speed, beat together remaining can of pie filling, dry cake mix, oil, eggs and brandy or cherry juice until well mixed.
g) Stir in chocolate chips.
h) Pour batter into a lightly greased 13"x9" baking pan. Bake at 350 degrees for 25 to 30 minutes, until a toothpick tests clean; chill. Before serving, spread chilled pie filling evenly over top.
i) Cut into bars and serve with whipped topping, if desired. Serves 10 to 12.

41. Cranberry Popcorn Bars

- 3-oz. pkg. microwave popcorn, popped
- 3/4 c. white chocolate chips
- 3/4 c. sweetened dried cranberries
- 1/2 c. sweetened flaked coconut
- 1/2 c. slivered almonds, coarsely chopped
- 10-oz. pkg. marshmallows
- 3 T. butter

j) Line a 13"x9" baking pan with aluminum foil; spray with non-stick vegetable spray and set aside. In a large bowl, toss together popcorn, chocolate chips, cranberries, coconut and almonds; set aside. In a saucepan over medium heat, stir marshmallows and butter until melted and smooth.

k) Pour over popcorn mixture and toss to coat completely; quickly transfer to prepared pan.

l) Lay a sheet of wax paper over top; press down firmly. Chill for 30 minutes, or until firm. Lift bars from pan, using foil as handles; peel off foil and wax paper. Slice into bars; chill an additional 30 minutes. Makes 16.

42. Hello Dolly Bars

- 1/2 c. margarine
- 1 c. graham cracker crumbs
- 1 c. sweetened flaked coconut
- 6-oz. pkg. semi-sweet chocolate chips
- 6-oz. pkg. butterscotch chips
- 14-oz. can sweetened condensed milk
- 1 c. chopped pecans

e) Mix together margarine and graham cracker crumbs; press into a lightly greased 9"x9" baking pan. Layer with coconut, chocolate chips and butterscotch chips.

f) Pour condensed milk over top; sprinkle with pecans. Bake at 350 degrees for 25 to 30 minutes. Let cool; cut into bars. Makes 12 to 16.

43. Irish Cream Bars

- 1/2 c. butter, softened
- 3/4 c. plus 1 T. all-purpose flour, divided
- 1/4 c. powdered sugar
- 2 T. baking cocoa
- 3/4 c. sour cream
- 1/2 c. sugar
- 1/3 c. Irish cream liqueur
- 1 egg, beaten
- 1 t. vanilla extract
- 1/2 c. whipping cream
- Optional: chocolate sprinkles

e) In a bowl, stir together butter, 3/4 cup flour, powdered sugar and cocoa until a soft dough forms.
f) Press dough into an ungreased 8"x8" baking pan. Bake at 350 degrees for 10 minutes.
g) Meanwhile, in a separate bowl, whisk together remaining flour, sour cream, sugar, liqueur, egg and vanilla.
h) Blend well; pour over baked layer. Return to oven and bake an additional 15 to 20 minutes, until filling is set.
i) Cool slightly; refrigerate at least 2 hours before cutting into bars. In a small bowl, with an electric mixer on high speed, beat whipping cream until stiff peaks form.
j) Serve bars topped with dollops of whipped cream and sprinkles, if desired.
k) Keep refrigerated. Makes 2 dozen.

44. Banana Swirl Bars

- 1/2 c. butter, softened
- 1 c. sugar
- 1 egg
- 1 t. vanilla extract
- 1-1/2 c. bananas, mashed
- 1-1/2 c. all-purpose flour
- 1 t. baking powder
- 1 t. baking soda
- 1/2 t. salt
- 1/4 c. baking cocoa

e) In a bowl, beat together butter and sugar; add egg and vanilla. Blend well; stir in bananas. Set aside. In a separate bowl, combine flour, baking powder, baking soda and salt; blend into butter mixture. Divide batter in half; add cocoa to one half.

f) Pour plain batter into a greased 13"x9" baking pan; spoon chocolate batter on top. Swirl with a table knife; bake at 350 degrees for 25 minutes.

g) Cool; cut into bars. Makes 2-1/2 to 3 dozen.

45. Pumpkin Cheesecake Bars

- 16-oz. pkg. pound cake mix
- 3 eggs, divided
- 2 T. margarine, melted and slightly cooled
- 4 t. pumpkin pie spice, divided
- 8-oz. pkg. cream cheese, softened
- 14-oz. can sweetened condensed milk
- 15-oz. can pumpkin
- 1/2 t. salt

e) In large bowl, combine dry cake mix, one egg, margarine and 2 teaspoons pumpkin pie spice; mix until crumbly. Press dough into a greased 15"x10" jelly-roll pan. In a separate bowl, beat cream cheese until fluffy.

f) Beat in condensed milk, pumpkin, salt and remaining eggs and spice. Mix well; spread over crust. Bake at 350 degrees for 30 to 40 minutes. Cool; refrigerate before cutting into bars. Makes 2 dozen.

46. Granola Bars

Ingredients:

- Pumpkin seeds, ½ cup
- Honey, ¼ cup
- Hemp seeds. 2 tablespoons
- Coconut flour, ½ cup
- Cinnamon, 2 teaspoons
- Artichoke powder, 1 tablespoon
- Vanilla protein powder, ¼ cup
- Coconut butter, 2 tablespoons
- Goji berries, 1/3 cup
- Pistachios, ½ cup, chopped
- Salt, a pinch
- Coconut oil, 1/3 cup
- Hemp milk, 1/3 cup
- Vanilla bean, 1
- Chia seeds, 2 tablespoons Coconut flakes, 1/3 cup

Method:

k) Combine all the ingredients together and spread evenly into a terrine pan.

l) Refrigerate for an hour.

m) When firm and set, cut into bars of your desired length and enjoy.

47. Pumpkin Oatmeal AnytimeSquares

Ingredients:

- Flax egg, 1 (1 tablespoon ground flax mixed with 3 tablespoons water)
- Gluten-free rolled oats, ¾ cup
- Cinnamon, 1 ½ teaspoons
- Pecan, ½ cup, halved
- Ground ginger, ½ teaspoon
- Coconut sugar, ¾ cup
- Arrowroot powder, 1 tablespoon
- Ground nutmeg, 1/8 teaspoon
- Pure vanilla extract, 1 teaspoon
- Pink Himalayan sea salt, ½ teaspoon
- Unsweetened canned pumpkin puree, ½ cup
- Almond flour, ¾ cup
- Rolled oats flour, ¾ cup
- Mini non-diary chocolate chips, 2 tablespoons
- Baking soda, ½ teaspoon

Method:

e) Preheat oven to 350 F.

f) Line a square pan with wax paper and keep aside.

g) Combine flax egg in a mug and let it sit for 5 minutes.

h) Beat puree with sugar and add flax egg and vanilla. Beat again to combine.

i) Now add baking soda followed by cinnamon, nutmeg, ginger and salt. Beat well.

j) Lastly add flour, oats, arrowroot, pecans and almond flour and beat until thoroughly incorporated.

k) Transfer the batter into prepared pan and top with chocolate chips.

l) Bake for 15-19 minutes.

m) Let it cool completely before taking out of the pan and slicing.

48. Red Velvet Pumpkin Bars

Ingredients:

- Small cooked beets, 2
- Coconut flour, ¼ cup
- Organic pumpkin seed butter, 1 tablespoon
- Coconut milk, ¼ cup
- Vanilla whey, ½ cup
- 85% dark chocolate, melted

Method:

g) Combine all dry ingredients together except chocolate.
h) Stir milk over dry ingredients and bind well.
i) Shape into medium size bars.
j) Melt chocolate in microwave and let it cool for a few seconds. Now dip each bar into melted chocolate and coat well.
k) Refrigerate until the chocolate is set and firm.
l) Enjoy.

49. Snowy Lemon Bars

- 3 eggs, divided
- 1/3 c. butter, melted and slightly cooled
- 1 T. lemon zest
- 3 T. lemon juice
- 18-1/2 oz. pkg. white cake mix
- 1 c. chopped almonds
- 8-oz. pkg. cream cheese, softened
- 3 c. powdered sugar
- Garnish: additional powdered sugar

h) In a large bowl, combine one egg, butter, lemon zest and lemon juice. Stir in dry cake mix and almonds, mixing well. Press dough into a greased 13"x9" baking pan. Bake at 350 degrees for 15 minutes, or until golden. Meanwhile, in a separate bowl, beat cream cheese until light and fluffy; gradually mix in powdered sugar. Add remaining eggs, one at a time, blending well after each.

i) Remove pan from oven; spread cream cheese mixture over hot crust. Bake for 15 to 20 minutes longer, until center is set; cool. Sprinkle with powdered sugar before cutting into bars. Makes 2 dozen.

50. Easy Butterscotch Bars

- 12-oz. pkg. butterscotch chips, melted
- 1 c. butter, softened
- 1/2 c. brown sugar, packed
- 1/2 c. sugar
- 3 eggs, beaten
- 1-1/2 t. vanilla extract
- 2 c. all-purpose flour

f) In a bowl, combine butterscotch chips and butter; mix well. Add sugars, eggs and vanilla; mix well.
g) Gradually blend in flour. Pour batter into a lightly greased 13"x9" baking pan. Bake at 350 degrees for 40 minutes.
h) Cool and cut into squares. Makes 2 dozen.

51. Cherry Almond Bar

Ingredients:

- Vanilla protein powder, 5 scoops
- Honey, 1 tablespoon
- Egg beaters, ½ cup
- Water, ¼ cup
- Almonds, ¼ cup, sliced
- Vanilla extract, 1 teaspoon
- Almond meal, ½ cup
- Almond butter, 2 tablespoons
- Frozen dark sweet cherries, 1 ½ cups

Method:

a) Preheat oven to 350 F.
b) Dice cherries and thaw them.
c) Combine all the ingredients together including thawed cherries and mix well.
d) Transfer mixture into a greased baking pan and bake for 12 minutes.
e) Let cool completely before removing from pan and slicing into bars.

52. Caramel Crunch Bars

Ingredients:

- 1½ cups rolled oats
- 1½ cups flour
- ¾ cup brown sugar
- ½ teaspoon baking soda
- ¼ teaspoon salt
- ¼ cup melted butter
- ¼ cup melted butter

Toppings

- ½ cup brown sugar
- ½ cup granulated sugar
- ½ cup butter
- ¼ cup flour
- 1 cup chopped nuts
- 1 cup chopped chocolate

Directions:

14. Bring the temperature of your oven to 350 F. Put oats, flour, salt, sugar and baking soda in a bowl then mix well. Put in your butter and the regular butter and mix until it forms crumbs.
15. Put aside at least a cup of these crumbs for garnish later.
16. Now prepare the pan by greasing it with a spray then put the oat mixture on the bottom part of the pan.
17. Put it in the oven and bake for a while, then remove it once it is quite brown then let it cool. Then next is to make the caramel.
18. Do this by stirring the butter and sugar in a saucepan that has a thick bottom to avoid it from burning quickly. Allow it bubble then after adding in the flour. Back to the oatmeal base, add the mixed nuts and chocolate followed by the caramel you just made, and then lastly, top it off with the extra crumbs you set aside.
19. Place it back in the oven and let it cook until the bars are golden in color, which will take for about 20 minutes.

20. After baking, cool it down before you cut into whatever size you want.

53. Twice-Cooked Popcorn Bars

Ingredients:

- 8 tablespoons cannabutter
- 6 cups marshmallows or mini marshmallows
- 5 tablespoons peanut butter
- 8 cups popped caramel corn or popcorn
- 1 cup peanuts, chopped
- 1 cup mini chocolate chips

For Topping:

- ½ cup mini marshmallows
- ½ cup mini chocolate chips

Directions

4. Heat oven to 350 degrees F.
5. Cover the bottom of a 9-inch square pan with parchment paper.
6. In a large saucepan melt the butter. Add the marshmallows and stir until fully melted. Stir in the peanut butter.
7. Add the popcorn and mix until evenly coated. Spread half the mixture into prepared pan. With damp clean hands, press the popcorn down and try to make even thickness.
8. Sprinkle with the peanuts and the chocolate chips.
9. Press the remaining popcorn mixture on top of the peanuts and chocolate.
10. Sprinkle with the remaining marshmallows and chocolate chips, and place in the oven for 5-7 minutes.
11. Allow to cool and then chill in refrigerator before cutting.

54. No-Bake Cookie Bars
Ingredients:

- 1/2 cup melted butter
- 1 ½ cups Graham cracker crumbs
- One pound confectioners' sugar (3 to 3 1/2 cups)
- 1 ½ cups peanut butter
- 1/2 cup butter, melted
- 1 (12 ounces) bag milk chocolate chips

Directions:

6. Combine Graham cracker crumbs, sugar and peanut butter; mix well.
7. Blend in the melted cannabis butter until well combined.
8. Press mixture evenly into a 9 x 13-inch pan.
9. Melt chocolate chips in microwave or in a double boiler.
10. Spread over peanut butter mixture.
11. Chill until just set and cut into bars. (These are very hard to cut if the chocolate gets —rock hard‖.)

55. Almond Lemon Bars

Yield: 32 lemon bars

Ingredients:

- 1/4 cup granulated sugar
- 3/4 cup cannabis-infused butter (softened)
- 1 teaspoon lemon zest
- 2 cups all-purpose flour
- 1/4 teaspoon table sal t

For Lemon Bar Batter:

- 6 large eggs
- 2 cups sugar
- 1/4 cup chopped, crystallized ginger
- 1/2 cup all-purpose flour
- 1 teaspoon baking powder
- 2 tablespoons lemon zest
- 2/3 cup fresh lemon juice

For Almond Mixture:

- 3/4 cup flour
- 1/2 cup sugar
- 1/4 teaspoon salt
- 1/4 cup butter (melted)
- 1/2 cup sliced almonds
- Optional garnishes: a dusting of powdered sugar, whipped cream, etc.

Directions:

For Lemon Bar Crust:

6. Preheat your oven to 350 degrees F.

7. Using a standing or hand-held electric mixer, beat 1/4 cup of sugar, 3/4 cup of softened butter and 1 teaspoon of lemon zest at medium speed for 2 minutes or until the mixture is creamy .
8. In a separate large bowl, combine 2 cups of flour and 1/4 teaspoon of salt. Gradually add the dry goods (flour and salt) to the creamed butter, sugar and eggs. Mix well until everything is thoroughly combined.
9. After the dough crust is mixed, prep a 9x13 inch baking dish with some nonstick cooking spray. Place the empty, greased dish into the refrigerator to chill for at least 15 minutes prior to baking.
10. Remove the dish from the refrigerator, and press the dough into the pan until you create a uniform layer. (Don‘t miss the corners!)
11. Bake the crust for 15 to 20 minutes in your preheated oven or until lightly browned.
12. Remove the crust from the oven and reduce the oven temperature to 325 degrees F.
13. Let the crust sit to the side for now.

ForLemon bar Batter:

9. Whisk together the 6 eggs and 2 cups of sugar.
10. In a food processor or blender, pour in the 1/2 cup of flour along with the 1/4 cup of crystallized ginger. Pulse the two ingredients together until fully combined. Proceed to pour the flour and ginger blend into a medium size bowl.
11. Stir 1 teaspoon of baking powder into the flour and ginger blend.
12. Slowly add batches of the flour and ginger blend to the bowl containing the eggs and sugar.
13. Whisk in the lemon juice and 2 tablespoons of lemon zest until fully combined and smooth.
14. Pour the lemon bar batter over the cooled crust, shimmying and jiggling the dish to allow any air bubbles to escape.
15. Bake the lemon bars in your preheated oven for 15 to 20 minutes or until the lemon filling has just barely set.

16. Remove the lemon bars from the oven and place them to the side for now.

For Sliced Almond Mixture:

4. Stir the remaining 3/4 cup flour, 1/2 cup of sugar and 1/4 teaspoon of salt together in a small bowl.
5. Pour in the 1/4 cup of melted butter, and stir the ingredients until they're well blended.
6. Add the 1/2 cup of sliced almonds, and stir once more.
7. Sprinkle the almond and sugar mixture over the hot lemon bars, and then place the lemon bars back into the oven for an additional 20 to 25 minutes or until they're lightly golden in color
8. Remove the lemon bars from the oven and allow them to cool in the baking dish on top of a wire cooling rack for at least 1 hour.
9. Cut your lemon bars into individual squares, and serve immediately with a dash of powdered sugar, if you so please.

56. Chocolate Bar

Ingredients:

- 1/4 cup butter
- 4 cups chocolate

Directions:

6. Melt the chocolate in a clean, dry bowl set over a pan of barely simmering water. If you want to temper the chocolate, add your butter.
7. Once the chocolate is melted (and tempered, if tempering the chocolate), remove the bowl from the pan and wipe the moisture off the bottom of the bowl.
8. Pour or spoon a layer of chocolate into your molds. Rap them on the counter a few times to distribute the chocolate evenly and release any air bubbles; then working quickly, top with any kinds of nuts, dried fruits or other ingredients that you wish and press them in slightly.
9. You can also stir ingredients into the chocolate, such as toasted nuts, seeds, crisped rice cereal, snipped marshmallows or other ingredients, then pour the mixture into the molds.)
10. Immediately put the bars in the refrigerator until firm. If tempered chocolate is used, it shouldn‘t take more than five minutes for them to firm up. Otherwise, the chocolate will take longer.

57. Oatmeal Bars

Preparation Time: 15 minutes
Cooking Time: 25-30 minutes
Servings: 14-16
Ingredients:

- 1¼ cups old-fashioned rolled oats
- 1¼ cups all-purpose flour
- ½ cup finely chopped toasted walnuts (see Note)
- ½ cup of sugar
- ½ teaspoon baking soda
- ¼ teaspoon salt
- 1 cup butter, melted
- 2 teaspoons vanilla
- 1 cup good-quality jam
- 4 whole graham crackers (8 squares), crushed
- Whipped cream, for serving (optional)

Directions:

4. Preheat the oven to 350°F. Grease a 9-inch square baking pan. In a bowl, put in and combine oatmeal, flour, walnuts, sugar, baking soda, and salt. In a small bowl, combine the butter and vanilla. Add the butter mixture to the oat mixture and mix until crumbly.
5. Reserve 1 cup for topping, and press the remaining oat mixture into the bottom of the baking pan. Spread the jam evenly over the top. Add the crushed crackers to the reserved oat mixture and sprinkle over the jam. Bake it for around 25 to 30 minutes, or until the edges are browned. Cool completely in the pan on a rack.
6. Cut into 16 squares. Serve, adding a dollop of whipped cream if desired.
7. Storing it in a glass container in the fridge will help preserve it.

58. Chewy Pecan Bars

Ingredients:

- Nonstick baking spray
- 2 cups plus
- 2 tablespoons all-purpose flour, divided
- ½ cup granulated sugar
- 2 tablespoons plus
- 2 tsp. butter
- 3½ teaspoons unsalted butter, cut into pieces
- ¾ teaspoon plus kosher pinch salt, divided
- ¾ cup packed dark brown sugar
- 4 large eggs
- 2 teaspoons vanilla extract
- 1 cup light corn syrup
- 2 cups chopped pecans
- Pecan nuts cut in half

Directions:

12. Preheat the oven to 340°F. Grease the pan using a nonstick spray and line with parchment paper with an overhang on two sides so you can easily lift the bars from the pan.
13. By utilizing a blender or food processor, pulse flour, the sugar, kinds of butter, and ¾ teaspoon of salt until combined. The mixture will form into clumps.
14. Transfer the dough to the prepared pan. Press it firmly and evenly in the bottom of the pan. Pierce the crust all over with a fork and bake until light to a medium golden brown, 30 to 35 minutes.
15. Using the same food processor bowl, combine the brown sugar, the remaining 2 tablespoons flour, pinch salt, eggs,

vanilla, and corn syrup. (Add the corn syrup last, so it doesn't get stuck on the bottom of the food processor.)

16. Pulse until completely combined. Turn the mixture into a large bowl
 and add the pecans.
17. Spoon the pecan mixture evenly over the baked crust. Place a few extra pecan halves on the top of the filling as decoration.
18. Place the pan back into the oven and let it bake until the center is just set 35 to 40 minutes. On the off chance that the inside still wiggles, prepare for a couple of more minutes; if you notice the bars are beginning to puff in the center, remove them right away. Put them in a rack and leave to cool before cutting into 16 (2-inch) squares and lifting the bars out.
19. Storage: Keep the bars in an airtight container at room temperature for 3 to 5 days or freeze for up to 6 months. They can be very sticky, so wrap them in parchment or wax paper.

CONCLUSION

The best dessert bars usually have layers of flavor and come in a lot of variations, the possibilities are endless, see what you can come up with!

Dessert bars also make a really nice Christmas gift or any other special occasion gifts for friends and family. Who wouldn't want to receive a beautifully decorated package filled with homemade dessert bars? That could be one of the best gifts ever! They have a pretty long shelf-life and can be baked a few days in advance. They can also be stored in the freezer if wrapped tightly in plastic wrap.

With thiis cookbook, you will definitely make your guests want to come back for another square to eat!

CPSIA information can be obtained
at www.ICGtesting.com
Printed in the USA
LVHW080737060422
715401LV00010B/421

9 781804 653913